Marvelous Minilessons for Teaching Beginning Writing, K-3

Lori Jamison Rog

INTERNATIONAL Reading Association

800 BARKSDALE ROAD, PO BOX 8139
NEWARK, DE 19714-8139, USA
www.reading.org

The International Reading Association attempts, through its publications, to provide a forum for a wide spectrum of opinions on reading. This policy permits divergent viewpoints without implying the endorsement of the Association.

Executive Editor, Books   Corinne M. Mooney
Developmental Editor   Charlene M. Nichols
Developmental Editor   Tori Mello Bachman
Developmental Editor   Stacey Lynn Sharp
Editorial Production Manager   Shannon T. Fortner
Production Manager   Iona Muscella
Supervisor, Electronic Publishing   Anette Schuetz

Project Editors   Charlene M. Nichols and Amy Messick

Cover   Design, Linda Steere; Photo, © Corbis

Library of Congress Cataloging-in-Publication Data

Rog, Lori Jamison.
  Marvelous minilessons for teaching beginning writing, K-3 / Lori Jamison Rog.
      p. cm.
  Includes bibliographical references and index.
  ISBN-13: 978-0-87207-591-7
  1. English language--Composition and exercises--Study and teaching (Early childhood) 2. Language arts (Early childhood) I. Title.
  LB1139.5.L35R64 2006
  372.62'3--dc22
                                                                                    2006025742

CHAPTER 4   109

Conventions: The Nuts and Bolts of Writing

CHAPTER 5   145

Revision: Making Good Writing Even Better

LORI JAMISON ROG is a teacher, curriculum consultant, and staff developer. She is the author of *Early Literacy Instruction in Kindergarten* and *Guided Reading Basics* and coauthor of *The Write Genre*.

After 17 years as a classroom teacher, Lori served as K–12 Language Arts Consultant for the public school board in Regina, Saskatchewan, Canada, where she was responsible for professional development and curriculum implementation in 64 schools. She has been a sessional lecturer at the University of Regina, teaching courses in writing process to preservice teachers. Most recently, Lori was appointed to the Saskatchewan Department of Education to develop a provincial reading assessment intended to guide teachers and principals in planning effective reading instruction and programming.

Lori has been an active member of her local reading council, has chaired the International Development Coordinating Committee of the International Reading Association, and has served on the Association's Board of Directors.

Currently, Lori is a private educational consultant who writes professional materials for teachers, consults with school districts, and speaks at conferences and other professional development events. She has presented at literacy conferences from New Zealand to Nova Scotia and San Francisco to Dublin. As a speaker, she is well known for her dynamic style and practical, research-based ideas. Lori's website is www.lorijamison.com.

Lori is the mother of one daughter, Jennifer, who is currently a university student. Her husband is Paul Kropp, the author of many novels for young people. She recently relocated from her "little house on the prairie" in Saskatchewan to an 1889 townhouse in the Cabbagetown district of Toronto, Ontario, Canada.

Author Information for Correspondence and Workshops

Please feel free to contact me with questions about this book. A link to my e-mail can be found at www.lorijamison.com.

MY DAUGHTER, JENNIFER, learned early in life that the best way to get out of trouble was to write her mom a note. That's why I have entire boxes of letters and notes that say things such as "To Mom, I love you, sorry for talking back," in a 5-year-old's print (see Figure 1). What Jennifer knew at age 5 is what we as teachers want all of our primary-grade students to know: that they have something important to say, that they can say it with writing, and that other people will listen. Our job as teachers is to provide them with the tools to achieve these goals.

Discovering How to Teach Writing

In my career as a primary-grade teacher and curriculum consultant, I have seen many changes in the way writing is taught. When I first started teaching, I taught "creative writing" as I had been taught—the once-a-week, one-draft wonder. I would assign a topic, the student would write the piece, I marked it up with corrections to spelling and conventions, the student made a "good" copy, and we would abandon it with relief on both our parts—until next week, when we started all over again with a new piece.

FIGURE 1. Jennifer's Note

In the late 1970s, the whole-language movement gave teachers a new awareness of the role of writing in literacy development. Pioneers such as Donald Graves, Nancie Atwell, Lucy Calkins, and Jane Hansen opened our eyes to the techniques "real writers" used and encouraged us to approach writing as a process rather than an event. Like many others, I welcomed the idea of writing-process instruction and writing workshop. Instead of once a week, my students began writing every day. Instead of writing single drafts, we planned, composed, and tried to revise our writing for publication. As a result of this new sense of process, my students were writing much *more*. But they weren't necessarily writing much *better*.

It took me a while to figure out the problem. Then I realized that I had been doing a lot of *assigning* of writing, but not a lot of *teaching* how to write. As Atwell says in her revised edition of *In the Middle* (1998), now I "teach with a capital T" (p. 22). If I want my students to grow as writers, I must set goals for their learning, provide explicit instruction on the elements of good writing, and expect them to be accountable for what they have learned. This is true whether my students are fluent writers or beginning writers just starting to put scribbles on paper. Teaching makes the difference.

The Purpose of This Book

I remember hearing the renowned Australian literacy researcher Brian Cambourne speak at an International Reading Association (IRA) conference. In essence, his message was this: Our students need to know how to read so they can learn about the world. But they need to know how to write so they can *change* the world. That is why effective writing instruction is so very important.

This book is about the explicit teaching of writing. I use the term *minilesson* as Calkins (1986) does: to refer to brief instructional sessions that focus on a specific learning objective and provide opportunity for direct transfer to the student's own writing. The 40 minilessons in this book offer suggestions for developmentally appropriate writing instruction in K–3 classrooms.

It is all too easy in the primary grades to focus on the conventions of writing—the task of taking our students from writing scribbles to letters to words to sentences. But there is much more to good writing. Even the youngest students can understand that good writing needs ideas, details, organization, crafting, revision, and editing before it is the best it can be. That is why I have chosen to group these minilessons into four areas: (1) topics and details, (2) substance and style, (3) conventions, and (4) revision.

Each chapter includes a collection of 10 minilessons focused on each area. I have drawn this collection of minilessons from my own experience with young writers and my observations of exemplary teachers in many primary-grade classrooms. All of the lessons are grounded in research and effective practice in literacy instruction. These lessons have been child-tested and classroom-proven. The scripts in the minilessons reflect the language I use when talking to beginning writers. The examples shown are actual samples of modeled writing. The teaching is structured to be developmentally appropriate, starting with what young writers know and stretching them to higher levels of development.

I hope many different audiences will find this book useful. The beginning or preservice teacher will find dozens of tried-and-true minilessons for teaching writing. The experienced teacher will likely find a few new tools for his or her teaching toolbox or a new twist on a familiar theme. Last, although writers in kindergarten to grade 3 are the main focus of this book, many of the book's lessons may be applied to students in grade 4 and beyond. I hope that the minilessons in this book will help you to find teaching ideas and strategies for students at all levels of development.

An Overview of This Book

Chapter 1, "Writing Instruction in K–3 Classrooms," examines the stages of writing development in the primary years. There is a great range of development in these years, from our kindergarten students, who are drawing and scribbling to "write" messages, to our fluent and proficient writers in third grade. This chapter describes the writing workshop and how it differs for students at various levels of proficiency, and it provides an overview of the powerful six-traits writing framework, including ideas, organization, voice, word choice, sentence fluency, and conventions.

Chapter 2, "Topics and Details: Getting Started With Writing," deals with the initial hurdles of generating and organizing writing ideas. These minilessons focus on encouraging students to find writing topics from the events in their lives, to elaborate on those topics with supporting details, and finally, to scaffold young writers in creating plans to organize those details before writing.

Chapter 3, "Substance and Style: The Writer's Craft," offers minilessons on style, focusing on precise word choice, a powerful writer's voice, and fluent sentences.

Chapter 4, "Conventions: The Nuts and Bolts of Writing," deals with topics such as "invented" spelling, punctuating dialogue, constructing contractions, and using capital letters. Writers know that writing needs certain conventions for a reader to be able to read it. These minilessons will give them tools with which to practice and perfect their editing skills.

Chapter 5, "Revision: Making Good Writing Even Better," shares several ways for students to improve the clarity and style of a piece of writing and presents a writing rubric in "kid language" to help your students assess their own writing and the writing of others. Most teachers would agree that revision presents the greatest challenges for student writers: Many children will say, "But I like it just the way it is,"—and they do. These revision lessons will show students that revision is simply—and painlessly—a way to make good writing even better.

What Makes This Book Unique?

This book has been designed to be practical and useful for teachers in several ways:

- Introductions to chapters 2 through 5 provide an overview of the lessons in each chapter, as well as research support and rationale for the lessons. Additional teaching ideas are also integrated into the chapter introductions.

- Minilessons are linked to stages of literacy development and the traits of effective writing. A chart at the beginning of each chapter highlights what each lesson is intended to teach, which trait it is linked to, and the developmental level for which it is most suitable. Teachers can use the charts to help them make decisions about which lessons suit the learning needs and levels of their students.

- Accompanying the minilessons are opportunities for teacher reflection; teachers can use the areas provided in the margin to write notes about each minilesson, which support reflective practitioners as they consider each minilesson and how they might adapt it in future applications. If our students are to master the writing concepts in this book, we will have to teach these lessons more than once. An effective teacher learns each time he or she tries a minilesson and then reflects on what worked, what didn't, and what should be done next time. These reflection notes also may be useful if this book is used for teacher discussion groups or professional learning teams.

- Minilessons are based on effective lesson planning. Each lesson includes a "before, during, and after" component—labeled Introduction, Instruction, and Application. The lesson introduction helps provide a link to what students already know and explains what students are going to learn in the minilesson. The instruction component is the explicit teaching aspect through modeling, demonstration, or think-aloud. The application component provides an opportunity for students to demonstrate what they have learned. Some lessons also include extensions, which are suggestions for developing the content further or applying the lesson in another way.

- Scripted dialogue shows the language that might be used in presenting these concepts to primary-grade students. Of course, each teacher will need to modify this dialogue to suit his or her students and individual teaching style.

In addition, throughout the book, I use the words *we* and *our* as a reminder that we all work together in our quest for excellence in teaching and learning. I am proud to say I am a teacher, both in my profession and in my heart. With this book, I invite you, my readers, to learn along with me.

The lessons in this book are not intended to be prescriptive or comprehensive. They are a "menu" of choices from which teachers may select or adapt to meet the needs of their students and address the requirements of their curriculum. My hope is that these minilessons will be springboards for further teaching in the writing workshop, as teachers try the lessons, reflect on them, and adapt them to suit the particular teaching situation.

CHAPTER 1

Writing Instruction in K–3 Classrooms

PICTURE A KINDERGARTEN class in your school. You probably have images of a range of students from quiet Emma, who is already reading second-grade books, to boisterous Alex, who doesn't know his alphabet from his elbow—and really doesn't care. In the average kindergarten class, students' developmental stages can range up to five years (International Reading Association [IRA] & National Association for the Education of Young Children [NAEYC], 1998). That range expands as students enter first, second, and third grades.

Literacy instruction for these diverse learners must be sensitive to the developmental nature of learning; that is, it should be based on a framework and associated benchmarks for progress, while recognizing that not all children will attain these benchmarks at the same time and in the same way (Teale & Yokota, 2000).

The Developmental Stages of Writing

To plan instruction appropriate to each student's needs, we as educators must understand the developmental stage of each student. Just as there is no value in teaching a child to walk when he has just learned to sit up, there is no point in requiring students to demonstrate literacy tasks beyond their developmental level.

Piaget (1952) observed that children go through a standard and consistent set of stages of cognitive development, and he cautioned teachers and parents to provide learning materials and activities that involve the appropriate level of motor or mental operations for a child at a given developmental stage. Piaget also pointed out the futility of asking students to perform tasks that are beyond their current cognitive capabilities. However, Vygotsky (1934/1978) postulated that there is a "zone of proximal development" between what a child can do with support today and what he will be able to do independently tomorrow. This "zone" is the point at which teaching is optimal. To provide the most appropriate instruction for each student, we need to be able to determine the phase of development in which the student is currently functioning.

The phases of writing development are not always discrete, but they are fairly distinctive (Education Department of Western Australia, 1994; Gentry, 1985). They have been defined and described in the research literature using a variety of labels (Fitzpatrick, 1999; Spandel, 1997). For the purposes of this book, I have categorized the stages of writing development as emergent, early, developing, and fluent. Of course, young writers may exhibit characteristics of different stages at any given time, and may even appear to regress into a previous stage on occasion. Our job as teachers is to assess and analyze what our students know and can do in order to extend their growth as writers to increasingly more sophisticated levels.

Emergent Writers

Emergent writers know that symbols on a page convey a message, although they have not yet grasped the relationship between alphabet letters and sounds, and may not even be able to distinguish between pictures and print. Most emergent writers draw with confidence and tell stories to go along with their pictures. They may even include scribbles, letter-like symbols, and random alphabet letters with their pictures (see Figure 2). See Table 1 for an overview of emergent writer characteristics and areas of instructional focus.

FIGURE 2. Emergent Writing Sample

TABLE 1. Emergent Writer Characteristics and Areas of Instructional Focus

Characteristics	Areas of Instructional Focus
• know that writing communicates ideas • use pictures to communicate ideas • may use scribbles, letter-like symbols, or random letters to add "writing" to pictures • do not connect letters and sounds • will role-play "reading" their text • do not understand that writing says the same thing each time you read it	• oral language development: vocabulary and storytelling • telling stories with pictures and words • alphabet letters and sounds • knowing and using the language of writers

At this stage, oral language development is critical, perhaps even more than proficiency with written symbols. In 1989, Sulzby, Barnhart, and Hieshima conducted a study of emergent writing in kindergarten. They reported that oral language proficiency may actually be a stronger indicator of literacy development than rudimentary use of alphabet letters. They found that children who write using low-level writing forms may actually be advanced in their literacy development if their oral language retellings reflect complexity and detail. For this reason, they recommend that oral language development be a priority for emergent writers.

At this stage, children can only read and write words they already know. Thus a strong speaking vocabulary gives young students a greater range of tools for reading and writing. As Elbow (2004) notes, this is the only time in children's lives that their writing vocabularies will exceed their reading vocabularies. Most adults can read many more words than they are able to use in their writing. Young children, on the other hand, have a very limited range of words they can *read*, but they should be able to *write* any word they can say because they are using their own symbols or form of writing.

One of the best ways to help our students extend and enrich their speaking and writing vocabularies is by reading to them. Ray and Cleaveland (2004) suggest that teachers "read to students often from richly crafted literature from a wide variety of genres. These readings need to be carefully rendered so that students can tune their ears to what good writing sounds like" (p. 18). Most emergent writers can *hear* and *recognize* the qualities of effective writing long before they can demonstrate it themselves (Spandel, 2003).

For most students at the emergent stage, writing consists of drawing a picture and perhaps labeling it with something they identify as "writing." The picture is an integral part of the message. Similar to the books teachers read that have pictures and writing, we can encourage our students to add "writing" to their pictures. This "writing" may consist of scribbling or random symbols at first. Teacher Sharlene Kramer's minilesson for the first day of kindergarten consists of modeling and practicing different "ways to write," from scribbles that resemble script to "book writing" (i.e., the kind of writing that others, not just the author, can read). Her primary goal is to get the children to put marks on paper to communicate a message, whatever form these marks take. This communication provides her with a means to assess what her students know and to plan instruction that extends their range of writing abilities.

Emergent writers do not plan, draft, and revise—they just write. Nonetheless, it is never too early to introduce a process and routine for writing. Cunningham and colleagues (Cunningham, Cunningham, Hall, & Moore, 2005) recommend five steps for emergent writers: (1) think of a topic, (2) draw a picture, (3) write something, (4) add your name, and (5) stamp the date. Students can count these simple steps—think, draw, write, name, date—on their fingers, and teachers can record these steps on a reference chart for even the youngest writers.

Learning how the alphabet works is a critical instructional focus for emergent learners (IRA/NAEYC, 1998). Just as all new learning is most effectively learned when it is connected to existing knowledge, alphabet letters are more effectively mastered when they are taught in a meaningful context. Reciting the alphabet, singing the alphabet song, or presenting letters in isolation in a "letter of the week" format only develops rote memory of the alphabet (Schickedanz, 1998). It is far more effective to teach the alphabet in the context of the most meaningful and important words in your students' vocabulary—their own names (Clay, 1991; Hall & Cunningham, 1997). There are many ways to build names into your kindergarten instruction. Chanting, cheering, and spelling students' names and then posting them on a "name wall" is a valuable routine for teaching and reinforcing alphabet concepts (Rog, 2001). Each day, a different student's name is posted on the name wall. When all the students' names have been added to the wall, the teacher completes the alphabet by adding common concept words to the remaining letters.

The name wall provides a reference for ongoing application of letter concepts. For example, if a student scribbles a sentence and tells you it says, "I went camping," you can draw his attention to the fact that *camping* starts just like *Corey* on the name wall and suggest that he insert a *c* for camping. Because the name-wall routine focuses on one name each day, the alphabet is presented quickly and concretely. Students learn the letters and sounds early in the school year and have the rest of the year to explore using letters in their writing.

Much of the instruction we do with emergent writers takes the form of modeled and shared writing. However, we do expect even our kindergarten students to write independently every day. While students write, I conduct brief "butterfly conferences" with them—circulating around the room and "alighting" briefly at their desks to offer praise and support.

Because emergent writers do not write conventionally, it's important to ask students to "read" what they've written or ask them to "tell me about your picture/writing." Then we can respond more authentically, usually with praise and occasionally advice, to "add some more details" to their picture or "use this letter" in their writing. It is a good opportunity to reinforce letter work and teach key vocabulary in the context of the students' own work.

At no time is the reading–writing connection closer than at the emergent phase (Elbow, 2004). At this stage, writing development often precedes reading development, especially with appropriate scaffolding. We want our students to construct meaning about how language goes together; by linking writing with literature, we can help them make this important connection.

Emergent writers—and all writers—should start writing on the first day of school and every day after that. By providing explicit instruction, opportunities to practice, an exciting array of tools and paper for writing— and the foundational understanding that they came to school to learn to read and write—we can encourage students to take their first baby steps to literacy. From these initial scribblings, we are able to make instructional decisions that enable students to experience success as writers.

Early Writers

When our students have learned to make the important connection between letters and sounds, they are considered "early writers" (see Figure 3). Early writers can put letters together to form words that they increasingly are able to read back consistently—even days after the original writing. They have a growing repertoire of high-frequency words and spell other words by representing the sounds they hear—sometimes with one letter representing an entire word. Most early writers still like to use pictures as a stimulus for writing, but at this stage, we want to encourage them to focus on the text rather than the picture. Table 2 provides an overview of early writer characteristics and areas of instructional focus.

Although early writers have mastered many concepts about print, most students at this stage still struggle with the concept of voice–print matching—that is, the understanding that words are discrete entities with spaces around them (Clay, 1976). Teaching students about word boundaries,

FIGURE 3. Early Writing Sample

or spaces around words, is critical at this stage, as students move from writing words to sentences to groups of sentences.

Instruction for early writers focuses on extending and building on ideas and getting those ideas down on paper with increasing mastery of conventions. We want early writers to add detail to their writing and to elaborate on their ideas over several sentences.

At this stage, we still want our students to "pretell," or explain what they plan to write about. Think about everything early writers need to consider when they write: what they're going to write about, what words they're going to use, what letters they're going to use, and even how to form the letters and place them on the page! If students can remove one layer of "working memory" by pretelling what they're going to say, they can devote more cognitive energy to the task of getting the ideas down on paper (Education Department of Western Australia, 1994).

Early writers have begun to make that essential connection between letters and sounds. Now it is important for them to be able to use "invented" or "temporary" spelling—that is, stretching out words to hear all the sounds and representing these sounds with letters. The process of using invented spelling requires young writers to integrate phonemic awareness (i.e., hearing the sounds in words) with phonics (i.e., connecting sounds with

TABLE 2. Early Writer Characteristics and Areas of Instructional Focus

Characteristics	Areas of Instructional Focus
• write more than one detail on a topic	• generating several details on a topic
• topics are generally related to personal experiences	• readable phonetic spelling (representing every sound with a letter)
• have many concepts about print, especially directionality	• conventional spelling of high-frequency words
• may not understand "spaces around words"	• concept of "word boundaries"
• connect letters and sounds	• revision by "adding on"
• have a small repertoire of high-frequency words	

letters). It enables them to construct knowledge of how language goes together, by experimenting, approximating, and generalizing with letters and sounds (Clay, 1976). Invented spelling is shown to promote phonetic knowledge as well as standard spelling (Burns, Griffin, & Snow, 1999; Gentry, 1985). This premise is supported by Clarke's (1988) findings that first-grade children who were encouraged to use invented spelling were more proficient in conventional spelling and word recognition than children who were not encouraged to use invented spelling.

Supporting invented spelling does not mean that we abandon all expectations for conventional spelling. A core vocabulary of correctly spelled high-frequency words is an essential tool in every writer's toolbox. The basic "glue words" that hold writing together must be learned to the point of automaticity so writing fluency is not impeded by having to sound out these common words that make up most of the reading and writing we do. Many teachers provide explicit instruction in a few high-frequency words each week and display these words on a "word wall" (Cunningham, 1995). "Word-wall words" are considered "no-excuse words"—that is, once they have been taught and displayed, they must be spelled correctly in all writing.

Because early writers can grasp the connections between letters and sounds, they are able to recognize that their writing should say the same thing every time they read it. As soon as our student writers are able to read what their writing says, they are ready to move beyond one-draft writing and begin revisiting and revising their writing.

Early writers begin to use a writing process: planning, writing, and revisiting. They usually plan their writing by pretelling and then begin to revise by "adding on" details at the end (Avery, 1993). Editing usually consists of ensuring that the high-frequency words that have been taught in class (i.e., word-wall words) are correct. Generally, students at this stage do not write more than one draft. Recopying teaches students little about writing and may even inhibit their motivation to write (Cunningham et al., 2005). Occasionally, when a piece of writing is going to be made public, we may have a student rewrite it; however, we must always weigh the time and energy expended on the task against the learning gained from it.

During the early writing stage, we see students progress from writing strings of letters to spelling many words conventionally and many more with logical phonetic spelling. They learn to separate words and use punctuation in sentences. They plan their writing by pretelling and revise by adding on. Most important, they discover the power of audience and the excitement of knowing that other readers can read what they have written.

Developing Writers

When students can elaborate on a topic using a combination of conventionally spelled high-frequency words and readable phonetic spelling, they are considered to be developing writers (see Figure 4). Table 3

FIGURE 4. Developing Writing Sample

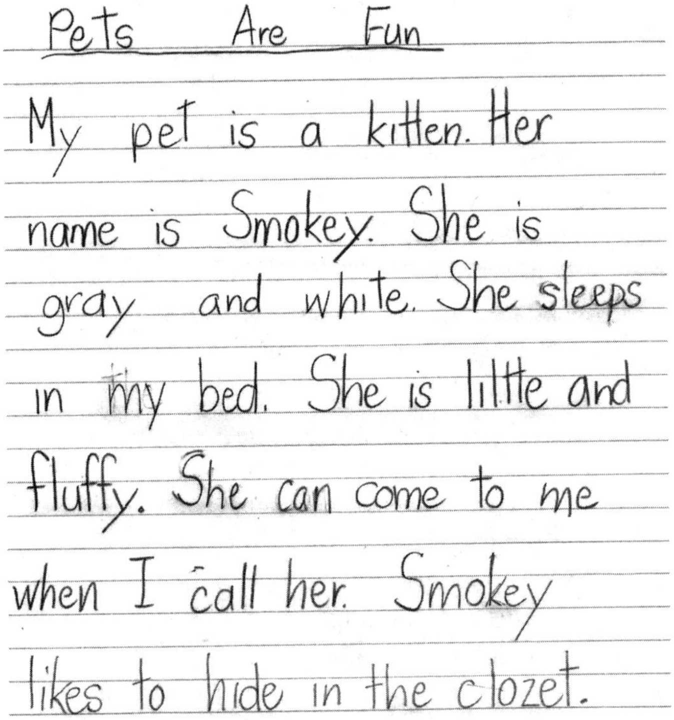

Pets Are Fun

My pet is a kitten. Her name is Smokey. She is gray and white. She sleeps in my bed. She is liltle and fluffy. She can come to me when I call her. Smokey likes to hide in the clozet.

TABLE 3. Developing Writer Characteristics and Areas of Instructional Focus

Characteristics	Areas of Instructional Focus
• write many details on a topic	• organizing information and details
• can write about topics beyond personal experience	• planning—beginning, middle, and end
• begin to experiment with description and word choice	• expanding descriptive vocabulary
• use mostly simple and compound sentences	• writing with personality and voice
• spell many words conventionally or with readable phonetic spelling	• spelling patterns and strategies
• use punctuation	• sentence combining

provides an overview of developing writer characteristics and areas of instructional focus. These writers compose extended texts and demonstrate an increasing mastery of spelling, punctuation, and grammar. Unfortunately, at this stage, writers may sometimes sacrifice craft for conventions. They put all their energy into making their writing "correct," and the writing may lose energy and voice.

Developing writers can generate an increasing quantity of ideas with more imaginative and varied content, but there may be a lack of structure or order to those ideas. It is as though the writer has put thoughts to paper just as they came to mind—a sort of "stream-of-consciousness" writing. This is a good opportunity to teach some prewriting techniques. Sketching a storyboard, brainstorming ideas, or completing a graphic organizer can help young writers generate and organize their thoughts before committing them to paper. Developing writers need to learn to put their ideas in a logical order, to group details that belong together, and to create a "shape" to their writing.

Guiding students to write for a variety of audiences and purposes helps them see that different writing forms have different organizational structures. This is not too early to begin teaching the structures of narrative, informational, persuasive, procedural, and poetic writing (Rog & Kropp, 2004). Units of study which explicitly teach text forms and guide students in practicing these text forms help students expand their writing repertoires and acquire an understanding of "writing to learn" as well as "learning to write."

Recognition of audience is an important milestone in writing. When writers think about appealing to a reader on the other end of the text, they are more inclined to consider style, organization, and correct mechanics to make the writing more clear and engaging. Teachers can help students find audiences for their writing in many ways: letters, pen pals, author parties, classroom bulletin boards, and publications for young writers.

Developing writers have mastered many of the basic conventions of writing. They spell many words conventionally—and many more words with readable phonetic spelling. Because they generate more text, they need more efficient supports for spelling. Reinforcing their knowledge of letter patterns (e.g., rimes, blends, and digraphs) and morphological chunks (e.g., prefixes, suffixes, and roots) helps them draft more easily and fluently.

At this stage, sentences are either short and disjointed or run on and on, joined by strings of *and*s or *then*s. By teaching students to combine choppy sentences using "linking words," we help them learn to add rhythm and fluency to their sentences. Sentence combining is a powerful writing activity; in fact, it is the *only* grammar exercise that has been shown to actually improve overall writing (Hillocks, 1986).

The writing process takes on increased emphasis at the developing stage. Developing writers plan their writing before drafting. They revisit their drafts and insert or change words or details for clarity and effectiveness. They begin to edit their own writing, fixing spelling and other conventions. And they create (more-or-less) "clean" published copies to share with an audience. Although developing writers still require a lot of teacher support for each stage of the process, they are beginning to take more responsibility for taking their writing from conception to publication.

Developing writers have mastered many of the foundational tools for writing. They know a great deal about composing and correcting their writing. With good instruction, a strong foundation in reading, and plenty of opportunities for practice, developing writers grow from technicians to artists.

Fluent Writers

The fluent writing stage, which extends from about second grade through adulthood, is characterized mainly by clearly organized and well-crafted writing (see Figure 5). Table 4 provides an overview of fluent writer characteristics and areas of instructional focus. Fluent writers are artists. Their writing has a smooth rhythm and flow created by varied and complex sentences. There is an evident transition from oral language structures to "book language." Fluent writers experiment with descriptive and figurative language as they think about painting pictures with words in the reader's mind.

Fluent writing shows increasing evidence of planning, with effective organization and well-developed content. Although fluent writers have mastered many of the conventions of written English, they may still experiment with spelling or sentence structure when they take risks with more complex words and ideas. The teacher's role with fluent writers in the primary grades is to continue to extend both their sophistication and their accuracy in expressing their ideas on paper.

FIGURE 5. Fluent Writing Sample

Earth Day

Yesterday it was Earthday, we went outside to pick up garbag on our play ground. We found alot of garbage. Stefanie found some glass. I liked cleaning up the school it helps the environment. I never pulote and I hope you don't.

At the fluent stage of development, writing individual letters and words places less demand on writers and they are able to attend more to writer's craft. They exhibit a strong voice, apply figurative language, and craft engaging leads and satisfying conclusions.

Fluent writers understand the process of elaborating on a topic, but sometimes their writing becomes unwieldy. Many capable writers have the impression that "longer means better" in writing; unfortunately, few students of any age can sustain focus and writing quality in texts that go on for pages and pages. Instruction at this stage should guide students in narrowing topics that are manageable and focused. Guidance in prewriting and planning can also help students write with more clarity. We can provide students with a repertoire of planning tools so they can learn to start with the end in mind, include key details, and avoid extraneous details.

TABLE 4. Fluent Writer Characteristics and Areas of Instructional Focus

Characteristics	Areas of Instructional Focus
• create writing that has a flow and sounds fluent when read aloud • write about imaginative ideas beyond personal experience • prewrite by using a variety of organizational and planning tools • access a variety of text forms for different purposes • use descriptive language and complex sentences • demonstrate a writer's voice appropriate to purpose and audience • have age-appropriate mastery of conventions	• increasing control of conventions • increasing sophistication in vocabulary and sentences • precise word choice energized by powerful verbs • figurative language • variety in text forms, audience, perspective • independent revision and editing • attention to writer's craft

Fluency is the operative word in defining fluent writers. Fluency refers to the rhythm and flow of writing. It is achieved, in part, by varying the length and structure of sentences. Most fluent writers have a sense of what sentences are and can write sentences of varying lengths and structures. Teaching students to "stretch" sentences by adding modifiers and prepositional phrases is one way to help them develop fluency.

Fluent writers also are encouraged to use powerful vocabulary. Fortunately, most fluent writers have progressed beyond the thinking that *very* is a descriptive word! Reading is the best tool for building literary vocabularies and attending to the techniques writers use. This is also a good time for teachers to introduce to students reference tools such as the dictionary and thesaurus to support effective word choice. From the addition of modifiers to the replacement of mundane words with powerful and precise nouns and verbs, this is the stage at which writers will discover the power of the well-chosen word.

Fluent writers still need instruction in the mechanics of writing. By assessing student writing, we can determine students' instructional needs, from subject–verb agreement to recognizing and using paragraphs, from the apostrophe to quotation marks. We need to teach these skills to students and allow students to practice them in the context of actual writing. Many experts concur that skills taught in isolation have little or no impact on improving student writing (Hillocks, 1986). Nor does it help them much if we use red (or purple, green, or whatever color) pen to mark every error. We want fluent writers to take responsibility for their own editing, and if we always step in to fix spelling or grammar errors, then students learn to rely on the teacher rather than themselves. Of course, there will be times when writing will be made public and we need to act as students' final editors; however, students should do most of the editing for classroom publication. Doing so may mean that sometimes writing is published with errors in it. It may be painful for those of us conditioned to think that "publish means perfect," but it is an important learning process for the writers.

We need to remind ourselves that the primary goal is not to create masterful pieces of writing; it is to create increasingly masterful writers. As a teacher–editor, I select one or two teaching points in each student's writing, then leave the rest for the student. I've found that if I try to teach a dozen things, the student quickly tunes me out. But if I focus on only two teaching points, the student is more likely to understand and retain them. The student then adds these points to his or her own chart of "things I've learned," to use as a reference for the next writing task.

Working with fluent writers is exciting and exacting. They need instruction just as much as our less sophisticated writers. Finding the right words to take students to higher levels is more difficult when the writing is strong. The six traits of effective writing, described in the next section of this chapter, provide teachers with the language to talk to students about their writing and are an excellent guide for assessing student writing.

The Six Traits of Effective Writing

Good teachers know that effective writing instruction starts at the student's developmental level and scaffolds the student to higher levels of development. It is a challenge to find the language to confer with students in order to enrich and extend their growth as writers.

One useful tool is the six-traits rubric. These traits, defined by the Northwest Regional Educational Laboratory (NWREL), include (1) ideas and content, (2) organization, (3) voice, (4) word choice, (5) sentence fluency, and (6) conventions (Spandel, 2003). This framework emerged out of a 1961 study by Diederich (1974) when he set out to determine exactly what was important in student writing. Based on his research, Diederich determined that the five elements most valued in student writing were, in order, the following: (1) ideas (relevance, clarity, development); (2) mechanics (grammar, punctuation, spelling); (3) form (organization); (4) wording and phrasing (choice and arrangement of words); (5) flavor (style, interest, sincerity). In 1984, Diederich's seminal work on writing criteria was extended by a group of teachers from the Beaverton School District, Oregon, USA, who worked with researchers from NWREL to redefine the criteria for good writing to those now commonly known as the "six traits" (Spandel,

2001). These criteria have been used in classrooms around the world ever since. Although "six traits" has become a commonly used generic term, in 2002 NWREL introduced the copyrighted term "6+1 Traits" to include the trait of "presentation," or the appearance of the text on the page (Culham, 2005). For the purposes of this book, however, I discuss only the foundational six traits.

The six-traits framework has been used in elementary, secondary, and postsecondary writing instruction for over 20 years (Culham, 2003). But only recently have we come to recognize the power of the six traits for beginning writers. The reality is that emergent writing in kindergarten and first grade is unlikely to show evidence of many, if any, of the traits of effective writing. However, it is never too early for teachers to begin discussing with students the things that "good writers do," examining with students the qualities of writing in the classroom literature, and demonstrating effective writing in modeled and shared writing experiences. Students will be able to recognize and talk about the traits of good writing long before they will be able to apply the traits themselves. As Spandel (2003) suggests, "At primary level, teaching traits is mostly about teaching language, giving students a writer's vocabulary for thinking, speaking and working like writers" (p. 7).

The six traits have always been a part of good writing. The work of NWREL served to define the traits in a framework that was accessible and useful for teachers and students. An essential component of that framework was a set of rubrics that described each of the traits at varying levels of quality. Since the original work on the six traits was done, many other educators have revised and adapted those rubrics to meet their own needs. The four-level rubric in this book has been adapted from the work of NWREL (Spandel, 2001) and revised for use with beginning writers in my district. I prefer to think of each level as a stage of development as much as an indicator of quality. For example, emergent writing will be at the lowest level for most traits, but this is more a reflection of where the writers *are* than how well they *do*. Our goals, as teachers, are to enhance current understanding regarding reading and writing and to build a foundation for future learning in these areas. Understanding the six traits provides a language and a framework that works for both goals.

Teachers can use the six-traits rubric in several ways. It offers a tool for assessment; this tool helps determine what students know and can do in order for teachers to plan what to teach them next. It provides us with a language to talk to students about their writing and what they can do to improve it. Finally, it helps us to set goals and standards for our students by providing a set of common expectations for good writing. Great writers do not develop in one or two years, but every great writer begins the same way in kindergarten and first grade: They struggle with letters, words, and sentences—just like the students in your class. Our job as educators is to help all students become—if not great writers—the best writers they can be.

Ideas and Content

What is the main idea of the piece of writing? Is it well supported with interesting and appropriate details? This trait, *ideas and content*, is more about *focus* than *quality* of ideas. Virtually any well-crafted idea can be turned into a solid piece of writing. It is the crafting and elaboration that brings strength to the idea. Sometimes our students will choose an idea, or topic, that is simply too broad to be supported in a short piece of writing. Culham (2003), one of the pioneers of the six-traits framework, notes that the trait *ideas* involves choosing a main idea, narrowing it down, and then adding strong details for support.

By teaching our students about the trait *ideas*, we help them "see the world as writers"; in other words, examine their own lives for topics of personal interest and relevance. Most teachers find that students write with more clarity, power, and engagement when they choose topics that are important to them.

Organization

The next trait, *organization*, is about the logical and effective presentation of ideas in a written piece. Good organization holds a piece of writing together and makes it easy for the reader to follow. It often involves "hooking" the reader with an engaging lead and wrapping up the piece with a satisfying conclusion. The actual organizational structure of a piece will depend on the text form and purpose for writing; for example, a recipe will be organized in a different way than a memoir. By teaching different genres and text forms, students will learn to organize their writing in ways that are appropriate to the topic and purpose.

Well-organized writing usually stems from a strong writing plan, so we want students to have a repertoire of planning and prewriting tools. These tools range from drawing and talking as a "rehearsal" of writing at the earliest stages to using more sophisticated graphic organizers and planners at later stages.

Voice

The next trait, *voice*, is commonly referred to as "the fingerprints of the writer on the page." Voice can be the most difficult trait to define, but it is the easiest to recognize. That's why it is so important to immerse our students in texts that are full of different kinds of voices—persuasive, humorous, passionate, peaceful. Voice is a combination of the writer's commitment, personal style, and connection to the audience. It makes a piece of writing distinctive and engaging. It may convey a range of emotions, depending on the author's purpose and the reader for whom the writer is writing. We can foster writing with voice by encouraging students to write about topics they care about and trying to show students how to make their readers care about their topics, too.

Word Choice

The trait *word choice* refers to the language a writer uses to express his or her ideas. Effective words are not just descriptive; they are precise. They are carefully chosen to deliver an intended message or to help paint pictures in the reader's mind. Beginning writers write whatever words come into their heads; as they become more sophisticated writers, they start making decisions about the most appropriate words to convey messages, stimulate visual images, evoke emotions, or compose verbal music.

Students in kindergarten to third grade demonstrate a great range in their working vocabularies. When young children make statements such as "I saw pictures in my pillow last night" or "The curtains gave me a hug," we want to help them capture the magic of their words in their writing.

I believe that the single best way to teach word choice for all students is to read to them. Listening to fiction and nonfiction texts that enrich students' vocabularies and demonstrate effective and precise use of language enhance all components of language arts development—reading, writing, listening, and speaking.

Sentence Fluency

Sentence fluency refers to the way the text *sounds* rather than what it *means*. Fluency is best achieved by varying the lengths, types, and structures of sentences. The result of this variation is writing that has an almost musical rhythm; it is a pleasure to hear this text read aloud. Effective demonstration of this trait is beyond the scope of most emergent and early writers. This doesn't mean they can't hear and talk about writing that "sounds good to the ear." Regular and frequent exposure to rhythmical text—both rhymed and unrhymed—helps students develop an ear for fluent writing.

Conventions

The final trait, *conventions*, includes the mechanics of writing: spelling, punctuation, capitalization, and grammar. Conventions are a courtesy to the reader to help them read what has been written. Primary-grade students vary a great deal in their ability to use correct conventions, and teachers' expectations and instruction should vary accordingly. The rubric presented in the following section indicates some general grade-level guidelines regarding conventions; however, actual learning goals for this trait vary from school to school.

Conventions exist for the purpose of making writing easier for others to read and understand, and they are most effectively taught as part of the writing workshop (which will be discussed in more detail later in the chapter). Research proves that drills and worksheets on grammar instruction actually have no impact on improving writing (Hillocks, 1986). I have found the best motivation for a student to improve his or her use of conventions is a *real* audience: parents, other students, the principal, the local newspaper, or others. When writers know someone will be reading their work, they want it to be as clear and correct as possible.

How to Use the Six-Traits Rubric

The comprehensive rubric presented in Table 5 is useful for both assessment and instruction. By "plotting" a piece of writing on the rubric, we can identify its strengths and weaknesses and thus determine in which areas instruction is needed at this stage in the student's development. The six-traits rubric also provides us with the language to talk to student writers about their writing and to guide them to higher levels of proficiency. The rubric is most useful during the revision stages of the writing process. Research proves that when students have opportunities to revise their writing based on specific and focused feedback, the quality of writing improves significantly (Hillocks, 1986). As described in chapter 5, even the youngest writers can engage in some form of revision.

Sharing the rubric with students can provide a powerful opportunity for students to analyze their own writing and that of others. Even the youngest writers can be taught the language of the traits to identify strengths and weaknesses of writing.

However, the rubric is *not* intended to be used for grading purposes. It provides useful *guidelines* for assessment—that is, for gathering data to improve instruction. Grading should be based on your students' progress toward the learning goals that have been set for them.

The six traits of effective writing are a powerful addition to teachers' pedagogical toolboxes. The traits provide teachers with new perspectives from which to view student writing. They offer language to use for conferring with students about their writing. And they guide teachers in making decisions about explicit instruction to take student writers from where they are right now to where they have the potential to be. The writing workshop creates an excellent organizational structure for providing that instruction.

TABLE 5. A Rubric for Beginning Writing Based on the Six-Traits Framework

	4	3	2	1
Ideas/Content	Focused main idea with interesting details and unique treatment of ideas	Clear main idea with some supporting detail	Minimal support for main idea; may have irrelevant detail	Limited content or detail
Organization	Well-structured organization; effective lead; adequate conclusion	Coherent, orderly structure, with some effort at lead and conclusion	Some details may be out of place; inadequate lead, conclusion, or both	Limited details; no lead or conclusion
Voice	The writing has personality; it speaks to the reader and may evoke emotion	Tone is appropriate, with occasional sparks of voice	Generally pleasant but not distinctive voice	The writing sounds "mechanical"
Word Choice	Consistent use of sophisticated and carefully chosen words	Effort at some descriptive words	Word choice is appropriate but mundane; mostly "conversational" language	Word choice may be immature and repetitious
Sentence Fluency	A variety of sentences with different lengths and structures makes the writing sound rhythmical to the ear	Sentences are correct, but most are similar in length and style; create a smooth sound	Mostly simple and compound sentences and repeated structures create a choppy sound	Writing exhibits an overall lack of sentence sense
Conventions	Superior mastery of conventions for developmental level	General mastery of conventions appropriate to developmental level	Control of most conventions appropriate to the developmental level	Inadequate mastery of conventions for developmental level

Adapted from Spandel, V. (2001). *Creating writers through 6-Trait writing assessment and instruction* (3rd ed.). New York: Longman.

The Writing Workshop and Minilessons

The writing workshop is a classroom structure designed to replicate the practices of professional writers as they take a piece of writing from conception to publication. Although a writing workshop structure may look different in different classrooms, Graves (1983) emphasizes that there are three common elements to writing workshops: (1) time, (2) ownership, and (3) response. Writers need regular blocks of time to give sustained attention to their writing. They need ownership to make choices about their writing: what they're going to write about, what form the writing will take, and whether or not they will take a piece of writing to publication. Finally, they need opportunities to share their writing and get a response from an audience. By using the writing workshop, we create a structure for our student-writers that aids in facilitating their best work.

Writers have various routines that involve planning, getting ideas down on paper, rewriting, rewriting some more, and finally publishing. In school, these routines are commonly referred to as "the writing process" (Graves, 1983). Although this process may vary from writer to writer and classroom to classroom, it usually consists of a series of activities that includes prewriting (planning, generating ideas, organizing ideas), drafting, revising (making changes to improve clarity and style), editing (fixing mechanical errors), and publishing (sharing with an audience).

The writing process looks different for writers at different stages of development. Beginning writers can talk about what they are planning to write, put their ideas down on paper in some form, and revisit the work to add details to pictures or "writing." As they gain confidence and competence, we expect them to go through more stages of the writing process and have a larger repertoire of tools for each stage, as seen in Table 6.

I have adopted the recommendation from Cunningham and colleagues (2005) that students should write three drafts for every piece they take to publication. For my developing and fluent writers, the "publication journey" involves planning and drafting three pieces in each writing cycle (see Figure 6 for a "map" of the publication journey). Writers select the best piece and put it in my conference basket for a revision conference (see TAG conferences, p. 27). Based on my advice, each writer must complete at least one revision to his or her piece. The student edits his or her own piece for conventions (see Be Your Own Editor, p. 141), and then has an editing conference with me. Only then is the writing typed or recopied for publication. The publication journey takes about two weeks for most students. There are many advantages to this process: Students learn to be selective about what they publish; keeping track of only three pieces of writing at a time is more manageable for both student and teacher; and at the end of the cycle, each student submits the three drafts and one published copy to the teacher for assessment and the whole process begins anew.

The writing workshop is based on the premise that writing does not always follow the same sequence, time frame, or process for every writer or for every piece of writing. It facilitates differentiated instruction by allowing students to operate at different stages of the writing process at any given time. While students are working, the teacher plays an important role in observing and assessing, conferring with students at various stages during the

TABLE 6. The Writing Process at Different Stages of Development

	Prewriting	Drafting/Revising	Editing/Publishing
Emergent Writer	Draw first, then "write"	Usually do only single-draft writing May use pictures, scribbles, letters, and letter-like symbols	Do not know that writing says the same thing every time you read it Will "read" or tell about their writing in "author's chair"
Early Writer	Plan by pretelling	Write first, then draw Draft using phonetic spelling Revise by "adding on" at the end	Fix "word-wall words" Can read their writing and will share it in "author's chair"
Developing Writer	Use brainstorming and organizers to generate ideas	Draft double-spaced and single-sided Revise by inserting or changing words and ideas	Can circle words that "don't look right" Need teacher support for editing Will recopy to publish
Fluent Writer	Use a variety of prewriting tools to organize as well as generate ideas	Revise by adding information in the middle or by cutting up and reorganizing text May start "cutting clutter" in text	Take responsibility for self-editing Will publish to share with a variety of audiences

process, and offering explicit instruction to move students to higher levels of development (Graves, 1983).

For all students, particularly those in the primary grades, the writing workshop should be a highly structured and predictable routine. Writing is a risky business because it makes personal thoughts public; therefore, we want to make the classroom environment as safe and reliable as possible. Fisher (1995) describes a successful first-grade writing workshop as having "a positive attitude of trust and commitment, an understanding of the process of writing, an orderly arrangement of materials, a predictable daily routine, and a clearly defined role for me as a teacher" (p. 66).

The writing workshop structure may look slightly different in different classrooms. However, most workshop sessions have three main components: (1) teaching time, (2) writing time, and (3) sharing time. The workshop generally starts with some explicit instruction, usually in the form of a brief minilesson (Atwell, 1998; Calkins, 1986). The largest block of the writing workshop is time for writing and conferring. While the students write, the

FIGURE 6. The Publication Journey

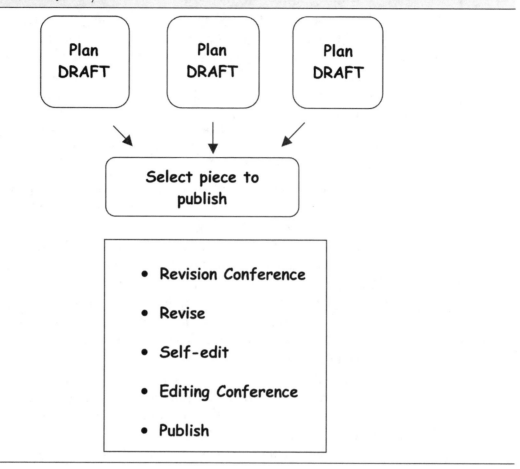

teacher circulates to offer advice and support or conduct individual conferences. The workshop usually ends with an opportunity for sharing, often called the "author's chair" (Graves & Hansen, 1983).

Given the importance of a predictable routine, explicit instruction, sustained writing time, and opportunities to confer and receive feedback from teachers and peers, the writing workshop requires a significant block of time, even for younger writers. A writing workshop of 30–40 minutes, for example, would consist of 5–10 minutes of teaching time, 20–30 minutes of writing time, and 5–10 minutes of sharing time. Although some teachers devote even larger blocks of time to writing workshop, this 30-minute minimum makes a daily writing workshop manageable for most school timetables.

Teaching Time

In the past, some of us misinterpreted the writing workshop as an arrangement in which the teacher functioned on the sideline, hoping our students would grow and flourish as writers simply by writing. Although this approach usually produced *more* writing, it didn't always lead to *good* writing or to much writing growth in our students. However, if we want our students to become more proficient writers, we must "teach with a capital T" (Atwell, 1998, p. 22), and offer explicit teaching that takes the form of writing conferences and minilessons for individuals, small groups, and whole classes of students.

Every writing workshop starts with teaching—that is, explicit instruction in an element of the writing process, conventions, or the craft. Because these teaching sessions are brief and focused, they are referred to as "minilessons" (Calkins, 1986). For K–3 students, and even beyond, minilessons virtually always use one form or another of modeled or shared writing (Rog, 2001). During *modeled* writing, the teacher thinks aloud as he or she writes, allowing students to hear the "in-the-head processes" that go on when a proficient writer writes. In a *shared* writing lesson, the teacher and students compose the text together while the teacher acts as a scribe. During *interactive* writing, students "share the pen" to transcribe the jointly composed ideas. Finally, *guided* writing involves students writing their own texts, with careful support and scaffolding from the teacher.

Almost any kind of enlarged print works well for modeled writing. Some teachers like to use an overhead projector because it enables them to face their students. Other teachers prefer to use large flip charts to keep the students physically close to the text. From a logistical perspective, it's a good idea to keep a bag of writing tools—with scissors, tape, and other necessary materials—clipped to the chart stand so precious teaching time isn't wasted searching for materials. Whether you use transparencies or oversized flip charts, keep those modeled writing pieces on hand to revisit for subsequent teaching.

With only about 10 minutes for teaching time, we want to ensure that each minilesson makes a strong impact. Based on research from experts such as Calkins (2003), Graves (1983), and Cunningham and colleagues (2005), as well as my own experience in many different classrooms, the following guidelines will help teachers to effectively prepare and deliver minilessons.

1. **Give the lesson a name**. Calkins (2003) suggests that teachers give minilessons "pithy" names that are meaningful to students in order to help "consolidate" the lesson. These names become tools that young writers can hold onto for future use. For example, in this book Bubble Gum Writing (see

p. 117) is intended to give meaning to the concept of "stretching" a word. I've tried to give all the lessons in this book catchy names so your students will remember the concepts involved.

2. **Keep it brief.** The operative word here is *mini*. Don't let the *mini*lesson turn into a *maxi*lesson. The purpose of the writing workshop is writing, so avoid the temptation to extend the teaching time at the expense of writing time. You don't need to finish a modeled text in a single session; in fact, it's a good idea for students to see teachers revisit an incomplete text to reread it, add to it, and revise it.

3. **Focus on only one key learning objective per lesson.** When you conduct a think-aloud during the modeled writing lesson, it's very easy to address a dozen different processes—sounding out some words, looking up others on the word wall, pointing out left-to-right directionality, using capital letters and periods, deciding which words to use, using spaces between words, and so on. Although it's fine to model more elements than you teach, it's important to be very clear about what you want students to learn from the lesson and be sure to focus on this learning with the students.

4. **Let the students know up front what you want them to learn from the lesson.** The minilesson is not a guessing game. Calkins (2003) suggests that you start each lesson by telling the students what they will be learning. For example, I might say, "Boys and girls, today you are going to learn about stretching out a word to hear all of the sounds and representing every sound you hear with a letter."

5. **Start by connecting the lesson to what the students already know or are already doing.** Students learn best when new information is linked to existing knowledge. For example, you might make reference to a previous lesson by saying: "Yesterday you did 'how to' writing in which you wrote lists of steps with number one, number two, and so on. Today, you are going to learn another way to tell the reader about the order in which things happen—using traffic-light words."

6. **Be explicit and direct.** Here's a radical concept: Not all teaching needs to be interactive. Sometimes you may want to involve the students in brainstorming or composing a text; at other times, you may find it more appropriate to simply convey the information directly. Make the most of a very limited amount of time for each minilesson, which requires making choices about the most efficient way to achieve the learning goals.

7. **Expect students to be accountable for their learning.** Sometimes the writing workshop will include specific assignments that apply a concept or strategy taught in the minilesson; for example, the teacher might say, "Today we are all going to write a special kind of poem that paints word pictures."

Often, however, students will move right into their workshop to work on self-selected writing. Establish the expectation that you will be looking for some demonstration of the learning during the writing they will be doing: "Today, when I come around to see your writing, I want you to show me a place where you 'pushed in' a detail."

8. **Plan minilessons based on what your students need to know**. Here's another radical concept: Not all students will require the same instruction at the same time in the same sequence, even if they are all the same age and grade. For this reason, commercial programs can't possibly predict what our individual students need at any given time, although they can provide you with good ideas and material from which to draw. Only you can determine what students need at a particular moment—and you get that information by constantly assessing students' writing to determine what they can do well and what they need to know next. You may choose to direct many of these 40 minilessons to the whole class, knowing that students will demonstrate their mastery of the concepts in different ways and at different levels. At other times, you may want to bring small groups together for specific instruction or provide a minilesson within an individual student conference.

9. **Once is never enough**. You cannot expect students to master a writing concept after one minilesson. (As we all know, some students will profess to have never heard of a concept we just taught last week!) By repeating a few lessons several times with frequent opportunities for practice rather than touching on many concepts only one time, students will be better prepared to master the habits of highly effective writers.

Writing Time

Writing time occupies the bulk of the writing workshop. During writing time, students write and teachers confer with students. Sometimes students work on assigned writing tasks or apply what they learned in the minilesson. At other times, students work on self-selected projects at the planning, drafting, revising, editing, or publishing stages. In most cases, the student is making decisions about how he or she will use writing time. An essential aspect of writing time is independence. Students must learn to use writing time responsibly, and not rely on the teacher for constant direction about what to do next.

I believe the most important routine of writing time is, "you're never done writing workshop." Students are taught that they have three options for writing: (1) start a new piece of writing, (2) finish a piece you started but didn't complete, or (3) revise a finished piece of writing. Even emergent writers can learn to start a new piece, add more details to a picture, or add more "writing."

That is not to say that "writing time" is exclusively for quiet, individual writing. During writing time, students may consult a reference book, read aloud a piece of writing, or confer with another writer. Writing is a social process for most writers (Roser & Bomer, 2005). Through conversations with others, students are able to gather ideas, clarify their own ideas, rehearse their writing, and plan for revisions. Ray and Cleaveland (2004) suggest that teachers separate "silent" writing time from "quiet" writing time. Some teachers play soft music during silent writing time. When the music stops, the students may move around and talk in quiet voices. One or more procedural minilessons will probably be needed to teach and reinforce the levels of noise appropriate during "quiet" writing time.

Writers basically need three kinds of tools for writing time: (1) something to write *with*, (2) something to write *on*, and (3) something to *store* writing in. (See Table 7 for a list of tools appropriate for each developmental stage.) Keeping track of several pieces of writing in progress can be challenging for young writers. A three-pocket writing folder, like the one pictured in Figure 7, can be a useful tool for collecting writing at different stages of the publication journey. The first pocket holds ideas and plans for future writing. The second pocket holds works in progress, or incomplete drafts. The third pocket holds finished drafts that have not yet been revised and edited for publication. These folders are simple to make, can be personalized for each student, and are durable to last from one year to the next. (See Table 8 for directions.)

TABLE 7. Materials for Writing Workshop

Developmental Stage	Something to Write On	Something to Write With
Emergent	A large spiral-bound scrapbook or drawing book of unlined pages, with plenty of room for drawing and writing on every page	Broad-line markers for drawing and writing
Early	A notebook or other collection of "half and half" paper to reinforce the separation of drawing and writing "Booklets" created from several pages stapled together	Blue or black pens for writing (to eliminate erasing) and markers or crayons for drawing
Developing	Three-pocket portfolios, with loose-leaf paper, preferably with colored lines to reinforce double-spacing (Accounting paper works well)	Blue or black pens for writing; bright-colored skinny markers for revision and editing
Fluent	Three-pocket portfolios, lined loose-leaf paper	

FIGURE 7. Three-Pocket Writing Folder

TABLE 8. Instructions for Making a Three-Pocket Writing Folder

Materials: one 24"x 36" piece of colored poster board, tag board, or Bristol board (as heavy weight as possible to fold effectively)

1. Fold the bottom third of the paper up to form a pocket along the bottom.

2. Fold the entire page into three equal vertical sections.

3. Label each pocket: "Writing Ideas" or "Topic Pocket," "Works in Progress," and "Finished Drafts."

4. Have each student personalize his or her own folder.

5. Laminate.

6. Use a long-armed stapler to reinforce the three pockets.

During writing time, the teacher's role is to circulate among the students to offer support, gentle nudges, and explicit suggestions for improvement. Conferring with students is one of the most powerful ways of differentiating writing instruction and improving writing proficiency because it provides us with the opportunity to offer individualized instruction at the point of need (Calkins, 2003). It is through writing conferences that we are able to offer the "just-in-time teaching" that helps our students grow as readers, writers, and thinkers. As Fletcher and Portalupi (2001) explain, conferences enable teachers to "stretch the writer" with teaching intended to take him or her beyond the piece of writing to improve "*all* the writing that student will do" (p. 52).

One-on-one conferences may take different forms and are structured in different ways according to the purpose of the conference. Master kindergarten teacher Nadine Benson uses the term "butterfly conferences" to describe the way she "flits" around the room and "alights" at each student's desk for a few moments to ask the child to "tell me what your writing says" and to offer support or suggestions. She may offer a compliment about the writing, a question about the content, or a suggestion to add a detail to the picture, add some more writing, or look to the word wall for support in spelling a high-frequency word. Other teachers use the butterfly conference to conduct a "status-of-the-class" survey—that is, they ensure that each student has a plan for his or her work, and they make a quick note of each student's progress.

Butterfly conferences occupy most of the teacher's time for emergent and early writers. But developing and fluent writers require more concentrated attention as they revise, edit, and publish a piece of writing (refer to Figure 6, p. 21 for the publication journey).

For many years, teachers in my school district have used "TAG conferences" (Cunningham et al., 2005; Rog, 1996; Rog & Kropp, 2004) as the heart of their writing workshop. TAG is an acronym that stands for the following: **t**ell something you like, **a**sk questions, and **g**ive advice. TAG describes a process for conferring with students to improve the clarity and effectiveness of a piece of writing.

Before a piece is published, second-grade teacher David Bird requires that the writer have a TAG conference with him and make at least one revision to the piece, based on his advice. He starts by offering specific and focused praise for the writing: "Your lead really grabbed my attention. It helped me hear the voice of the snowflake when you used that 'wow' word, *fragile*. Your piece made me laugh in the part where you were hanging upside down from a nail in the fence." This important step affirms what the writer has accomplished and makes him or her more receptive to hearing constructive questions and advice.

The second step of the TAG conference is for the teacher to ask questions about the writing. This stage empowers the writer and reminds him or her that there is a reader on the other end of the writing process. Asking questions does not imply a criticism of the writing; it simply suggests that there may be some aspects of the writing that are confusing or incomplete to the reader. The challenge in this process is to ask meaningful questions that will lead to a piece of writing that is more interesting, clear, and powerful.

The last step of the TAG conference is for the teacher to give a piece of advice—a suggestion that is intended to improve the quality of the writing and also to improve the writer. Sometimes the advice will arise out of the questions: "I think you should add in the part that explains how your dog got out of the yard." Other times, the suggestion may apply tools presented in a previous minilesson: "Add a 'wrap-around' ending or 'explode a moment.'" In David's classroom, this "advice" is not optional; if students are to learn techniques for improving their writing, they need to learn to go back into the work and improve it. He finds, however, that when the students know specifically what they are to do, they are usually quite willing to make the revision. (This represents a significant change from students' previous attitude of "It's perfect just the way it is!")

A student may request a TAG conference on any piece of writing but *must* have a TAG conference on a piece of writing that is selected for publication. An effective TAG conference requires preparation and thoughtfulness on the part of the teacher. When a student places a piece of writing into the TAG basket in David's classroom, David's homework is to read it and plan the compliments, questions, and advice he will give. This enables him to make the best use of in-class time and hold as many conferences as possible during the writing workshop. David's goal is to conduct the legendary "three-minute conference" (Graves, 1983), and he usually manages to operate within those time constraints. However, students do need to make the revisions that stem from each TAG conference.

A third type of teacher conference is the editing conference. This conference takes place after all revisions are complete and the writer is ready to publish the piece. Although a teacher might point out a misspelled capital letter or word-wall word during a butterfly conference, generally only work that is going to be published is edited. Teachers must determine which mechanical errors are within the developmental range of each writer. For teachers, it is always a "tightrope walk" between setting standards for correctness and encouraging students to take risks with language and structure.

Some teachers believe they must be the final editor for all of students' work so that all work is correct for publication. After all, professional writers have editors who proofread their work for them. But, as teacher Mit Lavelac points out, a professional editor is not a teacher. The editor's job is to create a polished piece of writing; the teacher's job is to help create a skillful writer. Rarely will Mit edit his students' work, depending on the purpose and audience (or how "public" the writing will be). But most of the time, he uses the editing conference to choose one or two key teaching points for that student to work on: a spelling pattern or strategy that they have already studied, a run-on sentence, or a misplaced apostrophe. His goal in addressing only one or two editing issues is for the student to learn and remember them. Ultimately, he wants the student to take responsibility for his or her own editing, which means that sometimes work will be published with mechanical errors. Experts such as Calkins (1986) and Cunningham and colleagues (2005) caution us that when we conduct the final edit of a piece of writing, we are taking the "ownership" of the writing away from the writer. Research shows that when students attend to their own errors, they are more likely to learn from them (Hansen, 1987).

Sharing Time

Ending the writing workshop with "author's chair" brings closure to the session by providing students with an opportunity to reflect and celebrate (Graves & Hansen, 1983). Some teachers designate a special chair just for this purpose. First-grade teacher Donna Burton also finds a microphone an indispensable aid for motivating readers and amplifying tiny voices. In her classroom, everyone *must* take their turn at author's chair; it is an expectation of their community of learners. At the beginning of writing workshop, Donna designates three students to share their writing that day. These students are responsible for selecting a piece of their own writing and practicing reading it independently. It may be a published piece or a first draft; it may even be partially complete, if that is the author's choice. The only rule is that it cannot be a piece they have read before. The important part of the routine is to practice so students can read their pieces with fluency and expression. For Donna's students, author's chair is a celebration, a time to praise and ask questions of the author. There will be other opportunities for constructive criticism during the writing workshop. In reality, most primary-grade writers will not remember suggestions made for future writing during author's chair; they just want to hear how wonderful their writing is. It is this kind of positive reinforcement that builds our students' confidence as writers and encourages them to learn and grow in their writing.

Good teaching builds on what students know and can do, and takes them to increasingly higher levels of achievement. When we know the developmental stages at which students are functioning, we are better able to provide instruction that is developmentally appropriate for all. The six-traits framework extends our ability to offer assessment-guided instruction by providing tools for scoring writing and for guiding young writers as they compose and craft their work. Finally, the writing workshop is an organizational structure that pulls the writing program together through explicit teaching, guided practice, and independent application. The minilessons in this book are based on these foundations of effective instruction.

CHAPTER 2

Topics and Details: Getting Started With Writing

RECENTLY, I WAS working with a kindergarten class on their writing workshop routines. At one point, I noticed 5-year-old Mark concentrating hard on his work, brows furrowed, marker pressing firmly into the paper. I wandered over to Mark and asked him what he was writing about. "How do I know?" Mark replied. "I haven't finished the picture yet."

For Mark, like many other beginning writers, writing begins with drawing and talking about their ideas. As teachers, we want to nourish that emerging literacy and help students develop a range of approaches to planning their writing. The minilessons in this chapter all relate to generating ideas for writing, adding elaboration and detail, and organizing those details in a coherent form (see Table 9 for an overview of the minilessons). Pick and choose those lessons that best meet the needs of your students.

One of the most challenging tasks for any writer is getting his or her initial thoughts on paper. Even professional writers sometimes find themselves daunted by the blank page. For beginning writers, the challenge is that much greater—not only do they have to think about the content of their writing but they also have to think about where to put the marks on the page, what words to use, what letters to use, how to form those letters, and where to put spaces. It takes a great deal of scaffolding and support for beginning writers to help them take baby steps in writing that soon lead to great leaps in writing progress.

In the past, many of us believed that students in kindergarten and first grade should not be expected to do any writing until well into the school year. The rationale was that students would not be ready to start writing until October or November, when they were familiar with classroom routines and had acquired tools such as alphabet knowledge. However, Martinez and Teale (1988) recommend starting writing from the first day of school, even in kindergarten—*especially* in kindergarten. Their case is a good one: When students are taught and expected to write on the first day of school, students simply accept it as just one more new experience in a whole day of new experiences. I have found that when we start writing on the first day of school, students rarely complain that they "don't know how to write." After all, most students will tell you that they came to school to learn to read and write, and that's exactly what we are asking them to do—from the first day of school and every day afterward.

TABLE 9. Getting Started Minilessons at a Glance

Lesson Name	What It Teaches	Developmental Level	Trait	Pages
How to Write in Kindergarten	Understanding different ways to "write" in kindergarten	Emergent	Ideas Organization Conventions	39–42
Tuck a Topic in Your Pocket	Generating ideas for writing and saving some to use another day	Emergent Early Adaptable to developing and fluent	Ideas	43–45
Writing Ideas Bingo	Generating ideas for writing	Early Developing Fluent	Ideas	46–49
Topic Tree	Narrowing a topic that is too broad	Developing Fluent	Ideas	50–53
"I Can Write a Book"	"Stretching" a story over several pages using patterned writing	Emergent Early	Ideas Organization	54–56
Sticky Dot Details	Elaborating on a topic	Early	Ideas	57–58
Five-Finger Planner	Generating and organizing ideas	Early Developing Fluent	Ideas Organization	59–61
Storm and Sort	Brainstorming ideas and sorting them before writing	Early Developing Fluent	Ideas Organization	62–64
3-2-1 Planner	Developing a prewriting plan	Early Developing Fluent	Ideas Organization	65–67
Turn It Into a Story	Converting notes from a prewriting plan into a piece of connected text	Early Developing Fluent	Ideas Organization Conventions	68–70

This doesn't mean that we simply hand out paper and pencils and charge the students to "go forth and write." We need to provide careful modeling, demonstration, and thinking aloud, along with sensitive scaffolding, to support emergent writers. The first minilesson, **How to Write in Kindergarten**, suggests a routine for the first day of kindergarten that honors the diverse literacy experiences that students bring to school. At the same time, it establishes classroom expectations for writing in kindergarten.

Unless your students come from a rich literacy background or have had strong preschool experiences, many of them will not know their alphabet letters, much less know how to form them or how to apply them to spelling. Nonetheless, all students have spent their lives in a world of print. They may not have books or newspapers in their homes, but they see traffic signals, business signs, television guides, billboards, and other symbols all around them. Thus, our job is to help children take what they know about print in their environment and apply it to their own reading and writing. This may mean encouraging scribble writing or using random letters at the earliest stages. "Scribbling" is a legitimate stage of writing development; it indicates that the writer identifies something called "writing" but has not made the connection between letters and sounds (Gentry, 1985). Whatever modes— pictures, scribbles, letters, or symbols—students have at their disposal may be used to express ideas in print. By encouraging scribbles or random letters at this stage, we help get students started in writing. Later, as students learn high-frequency words and letter sounds, these words and letters can be added to their writing.

Learning the mechanics of printing symbols on paper is just one "slice" of the whole writing "pie." Every piece of writing, great or small, must begin with an idea. As we support our students in getting started with writing, we want to focus first on content—generating ideas and getting them down on paper. Regardless of the writer's stage of development, these are the two main steps to getting started: (1) deciding what to write about and (2) elaborating on those ideas with details.

Sometimes teachers must assign topics for writing; for example, we may want the students to write a thank-you note to the bus driver, a poem for the school's holiday celebrations, a learning log in science, or a response to reading. However, giving young writers many opportunities to choose their own topics is equally important. A strong writing program should have a balance of prompted and self-selected writing. Self-selected writing is a vital element of the writing process (Graves, 1994). When writers choose their own topics, they are more engaged with the process and are more likely to write with passion, conviction, and voice (Brown, 1996).

There is one topic that interests almost every writer at any age: him- or herself. Primary-grade students in particular want to read and write about the ordinary events in their lives—home, school, friends, and activities. Freeman (1998) maintains that "primary-grade children are strongly egocentric and eager to write about themselves and what they know" (p. 25). Graves (1994) says that students must learn to read the world as writers, to look for a potential story in everything around them.

One way for teachers to support this process is by creating class charts of shared experiences that may be turned into writing pieces (see Figure 8).

FIGURE 8. Class Chart of Shared Experiences

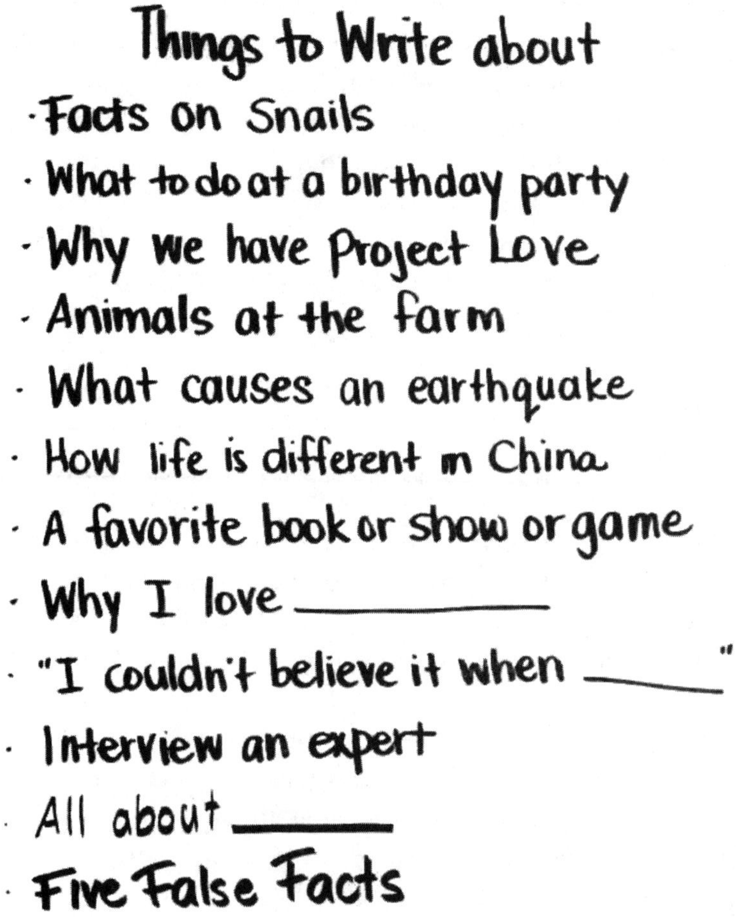

Things to Write about
- Facts on Snails
- What to do at a birthday party
- Why we have Project Love
- Animals at the farm
- What causes an earthquake
- How life is different in China
- A favorite book or show or game
- Why I love _____
- "I couldn't believe it when _____ "
- Interview an expert
- All about _____
- Five False Facts

Each time the class studies a new theme, takes a field trip, discusses an important issue, or celebrates an event, we can list the items on a "Things to Write About" chart. This chart also is an excellent record of classroom events and discussions. When we introduce new text forms such as procedures or reports, the class can generate new charts such as "Things We Can Do" or "Things We Know About." When the page is full, simply cut the ideas apart and put them in an oversized gift bag labeled "Big Ideas." (They're "big ideas" only because they are now on long strips of paper!) If a student is stuck for a writing topic, he or she can draw a "big idea" from the bag.

In addition to class charts of writing topics, students should have their own personal lists of writing ideas. **Tuck a Topic in Your Pocket** introduces the idea of "tucking away" writing ideas for another day. In addition, **Writing Ideas Bingo** helps students generate topics of personal interest by providing a series of sentence stems for them to complete—in words or pictures—in a game format. Even our youngest students need to understand that they have many ideas worth writing about.

As mentioned in chapter 1, a good writing topic is often more a matter of focus than of quality. Sometimes students may choose a topic that is simply too broad to be brought into focus in a short piece of writing. This is true for professional writers, too. In *A Short History of Nearly Everything*, author Bill Bryson (2003) looks for the small, interesting story in each broad topic. For example, instead of giving readers a generalized overview of astronomy, he tells the very human story of the discovery of Pluto. Students need to learn the same type of focus. Calkins (2003) refers to "watermelon ideas" and "seed ideas"; watermelon ideas are topics that are too broad and seed ideas are the "small moments" that lend themselves to a strong and focused piece of writing. To help students understand how to "skinny down" the topic or "branch off" from a broad topic to more specific ideas, teachers can use the **Topic Tree**, a minilesson on the graphic organizer.

Any topic may inspire writing; it is how the topic is crafted that leads to great writing. At first, most young writers simply write by labeling pictures, usually pictures of themselves. Patterned writing can support them in extending this range, and lessons such as **"I Can Write a Book"** help students "stretch out" a story over several pages.

Spandel (2003) asserts that young children can recognize and talk about the habits of writers long before they can demonstrate many of those habits. Therefore, we want to help even the youngest students develop and use the language of writers: *topic, details, draft, revise, word, sentence,* and *describe*.

One of the most important concepts is that of details to support an idea. **Sticky Dot Details** engages students in writing several details on a topic by placing a "sticky dot" at the end of each detail. Although the objective of the lesson is to build content, the added benefit is that it lays the groundwork for building sentences.

Finding a topic is the first step in any writing task. But the planning does not stop there. Writers need tools to help them clarify their thinking before putting their ideas down on paper. For most emergent writers, talking and drawing are the most important planning tools (Rog, 2001). Young writers know that pictures convey a message, and they are often more than willing to tell the story that goes along with their pictures. With support, these young writers begin to add symbols of various kinds, ranging from conventional letters to letter-like symbols. Some experts call this combination of drawing and writing "driting" (Hall & Williams, 2003).

Talk is an important element of the writing process for young writers. As Freeman (1998) reports, encouraging talking in the writing workshop can increase the quality and quantity of student writing.

Having emergent and early writers "pretell" what they are going to write helps them to rehearse their ideas and enables them to focus more attention to getting those ideas down on paper. Given the many demands on a child's cognitive energy—topic, details, words, spelling, letter formation, and placement on the page—pretelling removes at least one layer of decision making. This enables the young writer to devote more "working memory" to getting the ideas down on the paper (Education Department of Western Australia, 1994). Although we tend to abandon pretelling as students start to write longer and more complex pieces of writing, telling a story aloud can often be a means for even sophisticated writers to organize their thoughts.

An added benefit of prewriting discussions is that they may help a reluctant writer get inspiration from another student. Writers "hitchhike" on ideas from other writers all the time. For example, a student who tells about the time he fell off his bike might inspire another student to tell about the time he fell out of a canoe. Someone who says he is going to write an "all about" book on spiders might remind another student that she could write an "all about" book on bees. Thus, students can start with a borrowed idea and sprinkle in their own words, thoughts, and experiences to make it their own. As Graves (1994) says, we want our students to see the world as writers and one way to do that is to listen to the ideas of others.

The role of drawing as a prewriting tool changes as writers develop. For emergent writers, the picture is central and the "writing" peripheral (Cunningham et al., 2005). We encourage these writers to tell a story with their pictures. By the time the students have reached the early writing stage, the text begins to assume more importance than the picture and students are encouraged to begin to write first and then draw (Cunningham et al.).

Students do not need to abandon sketching or making a storyboard to plan a piece of writing when they reach the developing and fluent levels. At this point though, they can use other planning tools such as the **Five-Finger Planner** to generate details on a topic.

Effective writing is focused on a clear topic with details and elaboration (Culham, 2005), but those details must be organized in a clear and coherent way. Brainstorming before writing is a learning activity that is well supported by research in effective teaching (Marzano, Norford, Paynter, Pickering, & Gaddy, 2001; Tate, 2003). Although brainstorming can be an excellent way to generate ideas on a topic, it sometimes leads to disorganized, "stream-of-consciousness" writing (Rog & Kropp, 2004). **Storm and Sort** takes brainstorming a step further by helping students sort and sequence the brainstormed ideas before converting them into connected text.

Graphic organizers are other prewriting tools that support writers by organizing and connecting ideas to one another, supporting the writer in visualizing the "big picture" and enabling the writer to create a coherent structure for the piece of writing (Roberts, 2004). For reluctant writers, the benefits are even greater. Although a blank piece of paper can be intimidating to even the most proficient writer, an enclosed shape in which to jot a few notes may seem manageable for any writer.

Different writers and different tasks require different types of prewriting activities. Although some writers like to create a web of ideas, others prefer a more linear organizer such as a flowchart or story outline. The **3-2-1 Planner** is for beginning writers and has been adapted from the Four-Square Organizer developed by Gould and Gould (1999). The numbers 3-2-1 represent *three* key ideas, *two* details for each, all on *one* topic. When adult writers create a plan for writing, it is usually a sketchy outline to guide the composing process. Children, on the other hand, generally just copy what they have in their plan without much additional elaboration (Dahl & Farnan, 1998). The strength of the 3-2-1 Planner is that it forces writers to put details into the plan, so they don't omit or misplace key details or add details that don't support the main idea when they go to draft.

Although students can create a plan for writing, we cannot assume that they will automatically make the transition from listing ideas to composing a piece of connected text. The final minilesson in this section, **Turn It Into a Story**, demonstrates how to take the ideas in a planner and craft them into connected text. Because planning is an important step in the writing process, teachers need to help students stock their writing toolboxes with a variety of prewriting tools. A strong plan makes drafting easier for any writer and reduces the need for revision later (Cunningham et al., 2005). Prewriting tools do not limit students' creativity or oblige the writer to stick to a prescription; they simply enable students to "begin with the end in mind," not only shaping the piece more effectively but also enabling young writers to devote more energy to putting the words down on paper.

The remainder of this chapter offers a collection of minilessons for teaching students how to move from generating topics to organizing details to drafting a complete piece of writing.

HOW TO WRITE IN KINDERGARTEN

Developmental Level: Emergent

Traits: Ideas, Organization, Conventions

From the first day of kindergarten, we want to establish expectations that students will use drawing, writing, or a combination of both to convey a message. Many kindergartners, however, know nothing about writing and may never even have held a pencil, which is why we always begin with modeling. We use a think-aloud to reinforce the idea that the purpose of writing is to tell a story. This minilesson is a typical "first-day-of-kindergarten" lesson intended to demonstrate the various ways to write in kindergarten—from scribbles to random letters to conventional spelling.

Introduction: Explain to students that you expect them to be writers every day and that different kinds of writing are acceptable in kindergarten.

Boys and girls, one of the things we will do every day in kindergarten is write. [Show students a page from any familiar picture book.] The books we read in school have pictures and writing. And the work we do in kindergarten will have pictures and writing, too. Today, you're going to learn about some different ways that kindergartners can write.

Instruction: Start by thinking aloud about topics for writing. By generating two or three writing ideas and then choosing one, you may stimulate students' thinking. Following your lead, many students are likely to write about the same topic you chose. That's fine for now; however, eventually, you will want to extend their thinking.

First, I have to think about what I'd like to tell you about in my writing. What I'm writing about is called my topic. I could write about my cat Cookie or how to play soccer or going shopping for school supplies, but I think I'll tuck away those topics for another day. Today, I'd like to tell you about what I did on my summer holidays. That's my topic: "What I Did on My Summer Holidays." You know what I did? I went camping in the mountains. First, I'm going to draw a picture of me in my tent in the mountains. Here is my tent—and here is a picture of me smiling because I'm so happy to be there and waving out the door of the tent. Now I'm going to do some writing that says, "I went camping in the mountains."

Date

Observations

Notes for Future Instruction

This think-aloud helps model both the selection of a topic and the pretelling of what the writing is going to say. Next, demonstrate how to do the "writing." Recall that acknowledging scribbling and random letters honors the students' existing knowledge and ensures that all students will be able to participate at some level.

There are different ways to write in kindergarten. Today, we're going to practice three of them. One way to write is to do curly writing, which looks like grown-up writing. [Model writing squiggles or curls as you say slowly, "I went camping in the mountains."] Another way to write is with some letters. I might know some letters in my name. Or I might copy some letters that I see around the room. [Model writing random letters as you say again, "I went camping in the mountains."] Yet another way to write is to do book writing, which is the kind of writing other people can read. It looks like this. [Model conventional writing as you repeat your sentence.]

Figure 9 shows examples of these three writing methods. Before asking the students to write independently, teachers must have students practice each kind of writing on paper or on individual dry-erase boards. Students should have little trouble demonstrating "curly writing" and copying a few alphabet letters. Most students will even be

FIGURE 9. Three Writing Methods

How to Write in Kindergarten

PTLME
I went camping in the mountains.

able to write at least one word in conventional writing or "book writing"—usually their own name. Tell students that they will be learning lots of words in book writing as the school year goes on. This is an excellent time to teach them an important word in book writing.

You might not know very many words in book writing. Today, you are going to learn an important word in book writing: the word I. Book writing looks the same for everyone. When you learn a word in book writing, you will always write it the same way. It's a very easy word to write; it is a straight line with a little line at the top and the bottom, and it says I. From now on, any time you want to write that word I, this is how you should write it. We can mix up book writing and curly writing. If we know the book writing of a word, we should use it. [You may want to model the word I followed by some scribble writing or random letters.]

Have students practice writing the word I. This may be an excellent word to use to introduce the name wall in the classroom. From now on, when a student "reads" his writing to you and it includes the word I, require the student to spell it in book writing.

[As you circulate among students to confer with them about their writing, you might say,] I'm so pleased to hear you use that word I in your writing. And you know how to write it in book writing, so I'd like you to add it in right now.

Application: After students have practiced "kindergarten writing" and demonstrated that they are able to write in the "three ways," give them an immediate opportunity to apply their knowledge on paper or in booklets. It may be necessary to spend some time brainstorming ideas to write about before they begin. You may ask them to suggest things they did on summer holidays and provide some suggestions: Did you go for ice cream? Did you go to visit anyone? Did you ride a bike? Did you play in the water? Invite each student to tell what he or she is going to write about before leaving the group discussion to begin writing.

As soon as each student can tell you what he or she is going to draw and write about, give him or her the writing materials to begin writing. Some teachers like to make it sound like a privilege to get started:

Wow, that's a great idea! You'd better get started right away while it's in your mind. I'll be around to visit you soon because I'm pretty anxious to see your writing and hear your story.

Date

_____

Observations

_____

_____

_____

_____

_____

_____

_____

Notes for Future Instruction

_____

_____

_____

_____

_____

_____

_____

_____

Date

Observations

Notes for Future Instruction

The process of pretelling will only take a few minutes; most children will have an idea to write about. This leaves you with a few minutes to help the others get started.

Once this lesson is complete, students will have some tools for writing. However, remember that "curly writing" is just a starting point, even in kindergarten. As they add letters and words to their repertoire, guide students in integrating them into their writing.

TUCK A TOPIC IN YOUR POCKET

Developmental Levels: Emergent, Early, Adaptable to Developing and Fluent

Trait: Ideas

Students need to recognize that there are many possible topics that they can write about on any given day. Typically, students choose one topic a day, and save the others to write about another day. This minilesson uses a concrete item—a "topic pocket"—to reinforce the idea of "tucking away" the extra topics to use on another day.

Provide each student with a large envelope to paste into their writing books (see chapter 1 for a discussion of the materials necessary for writing workshop). The envelope is their "pocket" for tucking away good topics to use another day. If students are using writing folders or portfolios, the first pocket can be the topic pocket, as discussed in chapter 1.

The topic pocket may also be used to store pictures, notes jotted on a piece of paper, prewriting plans, or collections of ideas from activities such as Writing Ideas Bingo cards (see p. 49). Although this minilesson models generating ideas for the most emergent writers, students at more sophisticated levels of development will also maintain collections of writing ideas.

Introduction: Start by making connections to some of the topics students have written about in recent writing workshops, which will help remind students that there are many different things they can write about. Use the word *topic* to reinforce the language of writers.

In addition, it probably is a good idea to establish "writing partners" prior to the lesson. Use your own routines for random pairing.

Every piece of writing starts with an idea called a topic. Every day when you write, you pick a topic to write about. There are lots and lots of topics we can write about. I could write about why I love my Grampa or how I made a mud pie just like in our book Murmel, Murmel, Murmel [Munsch, 1982]. I remember the other day Jason wrote about playing T-ball and Kyle wrote about his new baby sister. [At this point, most students will want to share what they've written about. Take a few minutes to let them share their writing with the group or with a partner.] There are lots and lots of topics we can write about, but we can only write about one at a time! I don't want to forget all those other ideas because I might want to write about them

Date

Observations

Notes for Future Instruction

another time. So I'm going to show you how you can use a topic pocket to tuck away those extra ideas and save them for another day.

Instruction: Help students begin to generate topics for the topic pocket by giving each student a sheet of paper divided into four sections. Tell students that in each square they will draw a "quick pic," or a sketch with just enough detail for the student to remember what the picture represents.

Close your eyes for one minute and take a picture in your mind of a person who is very important to you. Turn to the person beside you and tell him or her who your special person is. I'm going to give you two minutes to draw a quick pic of that person in the first box. Remember that a quick pic doesn't have a lot of details; it has just enough detail to help you remember what you drew when you look at this paper tomorrow or another day.

Model how you would draw a quick pic of a favorite person (see Figure 10), and then allow two minutes for students to sketch their own favorite person.

FIGURE 10. Quick Pic Sample

Continue the process with the remaining three boxes, telling students to think about and draw (1) a special place they like to go, (2) a particular food they love to eat, and (3) something they like to do. Provide students with an opportunity to draw and to talk about their pictures as they draw. After they have completed all four sketches, tell the students that these are four topics they can write about.

Now you have four pictures that could be topics for writing. [Point to each picture on your model.] I might write about my Gramps, going swimming, camping in the mountains, or my favorite food—spaghetti and meatballs. I think today I'm going to write about going swimming, and I'm going to tuck those other ideas away to use for another day.

After thinking aloud as you choose a topic, model for the students how you use another paper to draw a detailed picture and add some writing.

Application: Have the students choose one of their topics to draw and write about in their writing books or folders today and tuck the others away for another day. Before tucking them into the topic pocket, you may choose to cut the page into four squares so each topic is on a separate piece of paper. Even if students can't remember what they drew, the activity still reinforces the concept of generating several ideas, choosing one to write about, and tucking away the others to use another day.

Extension: Other ways to generate topics to tuck away including the following:

- If you brainstorm lists of ideas to write about with the students (e.g., "Things to Write About" chart, "Things We Can Do" chart, or "Things We Know About" chart), have each student choose two or three topics from the charts that they can "make their own" and tuck into the topic pocket.
- Tell students to be on the lookout for topics they might write about. They can always jot down an idea and tuck it into their pocket to use during writing time.
- Students can insert photographs in their topic pockets. Students may bring photographs from home, or you may provide them with photographs from school events.

Date

Observations

Notes for Future Instruction

Date

Observations

Notes for Future Instruction

WRITING IDEAS BINGO

Developmental Levels: Early, Developing, Fluent

Trait: Ideas

Writing Ideas Bingo is intended to help students generate topics of personal interest by completing a series of sentence stems on a card with grids. Each completed sentence can be a potential writing topic. We call it Bingo because students are invited to shout "Bingo!" when they "black out" the card by completing every sentence stem. (The perception that this lesson is a game helps motivate otherwise reluctant writers.) However, the activity should be structured to ensure that all students have an opportunity to complete the card and shout "Bingo!" The goal is to have your students generate a collection of topics of personal significance to tuck into their topic pockets.

This activity may be adapted for less sophisticated writers by reducing the number of squares on the Bingo card, reading aloud the sentence stems to the students, or having students draw a picture in each box in order to complete the stems. Students also may be asked to complete only part of the card at one time. For example, you might tell students that they can shout "Bingo!" after they have completed any four squares.

Introduction: Connect this lesson to previous discussions of writing topics.

Some days, it's easy to think of topics to write about. In fact, some days, we have a topic we're just itching to write about! But other days, it's hard. That's why most writers have a collection of writing topics saved up for those days when they just can't think of anything to write about. The first pocket in your writing folder gives you a place where you can tuck away those ideas that you're saving for another day.

Today, we're going to play a game that will help you think of some writing ideas that you care about. Then you will tuck them away in your topic pocket for a day when you need a writing topic.

Instruction: Photocopy for each student the Bingo card found at the end of the minilesson, or create your own. Make an overhead transparency of the card to use as you demonstrate how to complete it. As you model, read each of the topics on the card and demonstrate how you complete each sentence stem with a phrase of a few words.

Tell the students they may leave the middle box blank because it is a "free" square. They will fill in that square later.

We're going to play a game called Writing Ideas Bingo to help us think of some writing topics to tuck away in our writing folders. The way you play the game is to think of a few words to complete the sentence in each box. When you have finished all the boxes, you have "blacked out" the Bingo card and you can call "Bingo!" Let me show you how I do it. As I show you my ideas, you might want to think about what you will write on your own Bingo card.

Application: Provide each student with a copy of the Bingo card. At your signal, have students begin completing the sentence stems in each square. It's important to allow enough time for all students to complete *most* of the card; you might hear dozens of "Bingos!" before you move on. For those students who finish quickly, it's a good idea to have some "when you're done" activities in place such as the following:

- List five things you love and five things you dislike.
- List five topics you're an expert on.
- Write the letters in your name in a column. For each letter, write one thing you know about or know how to do that begins with each letter.
- Draw a border around your page that shows things you are good at or interested in.

When you feel the students have had adequate time to complete their Bingo cards, go around the room in "round-robin" style and ask each student to share one idea from his or her card. Instruct the students that the blank box in the middle of the card will be used to "get an idea" from another writer. Students should fill in the center box as they get an idea from listening to the other students read their ideas. Have students choose one topic to write about that day and then tuck the completed Bingo cards into their topic pockets. Remind students that any of these sentences can become the topic for a piece of writing in the future. In the future, you may want to assign a topic from the Bingo card as a reminder to students to use the ideas in their topic pockets.

Extension: This activity may be repeated at other times of the year with different sentence stems. For example, if you are teaching a unit on

Date

Observations

Notes for Future Instruction

informational writing, you might create a Bingo card with stems such as the following:

- An animal I would like to learn more about is...
- A place I would like to learn more about is...
- An important person I would like to learn more about is...
- An invention I would like to learn more about is...
- A bird I would like to learn more about is...
- A sea creature I would like to learn more about is...
- A topic about space I would like to learn more about is...
- A topic about weather I would like to learn more about is...

If you are presenting a unit on procedural writing, you might create a Bingo card with stems such as the following:

- A game I know how to play is...
- A food I know how to make is...
- A place I know how to get to is...
- A craft I know how to do is...
- A funny thing I know how to do is...

Writing Ideas Bingo Card

I had so much fun when...	I was really scared when...	I couldn't believe it when...
I got this scar from...		When I was little...
It wasn't fair when...	I laughed so hard when...	I was so mad when...

NOTES

Date

_____

Observations

_____
_____
_____
_____
_____
_____
_____
_____
_____

Notes for Future Instruction

_____
_____
_____
_____
_____
_____
_____
_____
_____
_____
_____

TOPIC TREE

Developmental Levels: Developing, Fluent

Trait: Ideas

Sometimes students select topics that are just too broad for focused writing. The Topic Tree is a graphic organizer that helps young writers focus their topic by providing a visual representation of "branching off" from the main topic into more specific topics. The lesson also directs students to think about their audience and consider what the reader might want to know about this topic.

The minilesson described in the following example addresses personal writing, but this activity is also useful for focusing a topic for informational writing.

Introduction: Connect this lesson to students' background knowledge on selecting topics. Discuss the difficulties of writing when a topic is simply "too big." If possible, use a piece of existing writing (or create a new piece) for demonstration purposes.

I have been reading about many interesting topics in your writing. Sometimes writers want to write about great big topics like "My Trip to Florida." The problem with a topic like that is there are too many details to tell in one piece of writing. Look at the following piece of writing that a student from another class wrote:

> My Trip to Florida
>
> My family went to Florida for Spring Break. We had to get up early in the morning to go to the airport. I got to sit in Seat 6D on the plane. The lady brought me some snacks and something to drink. I looked out over the clouds till the plane landed in Orlando. When we got there, my family rented a brown van. We stayed in a hotel that looked like a castle. We went to Epcot Center and Magic Kingdom. I can hardly wait to go back to Florida again.

This writer has written some details about the plane and the hotel and what she saw. But she's tried to cover too much so she hasn't told enough about the really interesting parts. As a reader, I'm not that interested in what seat she had on the plane or what color the van was. But I'd sure like to know about what she saw at Epcot or Magic Kingdom. I think she needs to "skinny down" her topic a bit. Instead of telling us everything that happened, she needs to tell about just one thing and then add more details about that one thing.

Today, you're going to learn how to "skinny down" a topic that is too big using a Topic Tree.

Instruction: Model for the students how to complete the Topic Tree with a topic of your choice, or use the example provided (see Figure 11).

I would like to skinny down the great big topic of "My Trip to Florida." I'm going to use this Topic Tree to help me. My great big topic is like the trunk of the tree, so I'm going to write "My Trip to Florida" on the trunk.

FIGURE 11. Topic Tree Sample

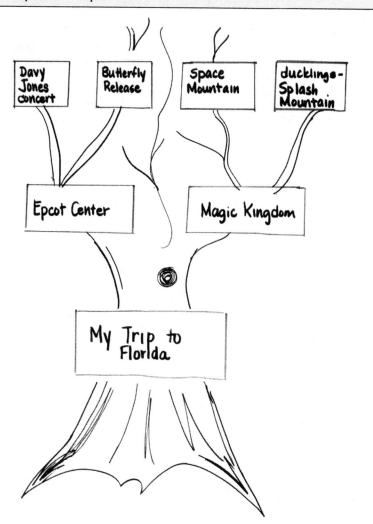

Now, let's see how I could branch that big topic into two little topics: Magic Kingdom and Epcot Center. Each one of these is a little easier to write about.

Maybe I can branch it off even more. I might write about the butterfly release at Epcot or the Davy Jones concert. Or I could branch off the Magic Kingdom topic and write about the Space Mountain ride or the Splash Mountain ride.

Branching off again, I could write about finding the little ducklings floating in the Splash Mountain ride and how I scooped them up out of the water so they wouldn't get squished by the logs. Now I've found the story I want to tell! I can put lots of details into this story. Not only that, I've got three more story ideas to tuck away in my topic pocket to use for another day.

Application: Have students work in pairs to complete a Topic Tree on a common topic. Photocopy the Topic Tree on the next page and provide each pair of students with a copy of it for guided practice. Have them practice skinnying down a great big topic such as "Animals" or "My Second-Grade Year." They can tuck these Topic Trees into their topic pockets to use in a piece of writing on another day.

Topic Tree

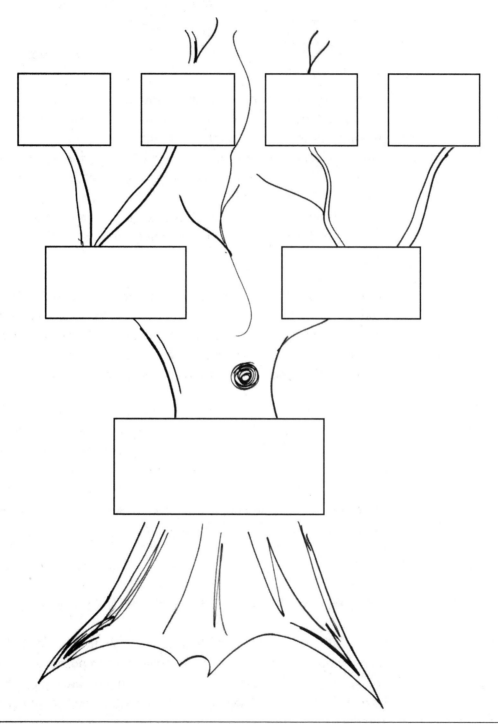

"I CAN WRITE A BOOK"

Developmental Levels: Emergent, Early

Traits: Ideas, Organization

Although students should not rely on formulas for writing, sometimes providing students with writing patterns and frameworks can help stimulate ideas for writing, introduce different structures for writing, and build confidence for reluctant writers. Patterned writing with beginning writers is a good way to demonstrate how to "stretch out" a piece of writing over several pages.

The lesson presented here is for emergent or early writers. Patterned writing may be also used with developing and fluent writers for specific purposes.

Introduction: Connecting this lesson to students' experiences with guided reading texts is effective because these texts are patterned and predictable at this stage of literacy development. Revisit a familiar pattern book by reading it aloud or as a shared reading activity. (A predictable big book also can serve the same purpose.)

The author of the book Sun Fun, Elle Ruth Orav (2001), used a pattern to write her book. Each page starts with "I can put on my..." (see Figure 12A and B). Today, you're going to learn how you can write a book like this one—one that "stretches" over several pages.

Instruction: Review the book you have chosen, and invite students to use the pattern to create their own writing.

Elle Ruth Orav's book is all about what you put on to go out in the sun. Let's make our own book about what we put on to go out in the snow. Here is the pattern that we will use for each page: "I can put on my...."

Staple four pages together to use as a demonstration booklet. Using a shared writing format, have the students help compose the text while you act as scribe and write each sentence on a separate page. Model how to add an illustration after you have written the text on each page. The purpose of this exercise is to focus on the text and then draw afterward.

FIGURE 12A AND B. Pattern Book Pages

A

I can put on my sunglasses.

B

I can put on my t-shirt.

From Orav, E.R. (2001). *Sun fun.* Ill. L. Quach. Toronto, ON: Curriculum Plus. Reprinted with permission.

Application: Give each student a four-page booklet to create his or her own pattern book. The first time students complete this activity, you may want to provide a photocopy of the patterned text for each student, which will enable them to focus on their own writing rather than copying the existing text. (See Table 10 for possible pattern ideas for this activity.) It may be necessary to brainstorm some potential ideas for adding to the text. Gradually decrease the support you give students as they work on more pattern books.

N O T E S

Date

_____

Observations

_____
_____
_____
_____
_____
_____
_____
_____
_____

Notes for Future Instruction

_____
_____
_____
_____
_____
_____
_____
_____

TABLE 10. Ideas for Pattern Books

I can...	I am thankful for...
I like/love...	Dear Santa, thanks for the...
I don't like...	When I'm seven...
I saw...	Things I like
I am...	Things that are red
I am good at...	All about cats
After school, I like to...	At the zoo, you can see...
I went to...	At Halloween, you can see...
I like to eat...	My feet can...
I would like a...	My family is...
If I could, I would...	Ice cream is...
In my garden, I would plant...	

Many ideas for predictable books and charts also may be found in Hall, D.P., & Cunningham, P.M. (1997). *Month-by-month reading, writing, and phonics for kindergarten: Systematic, multilevel instruction for kindergarten.* Greensboro, NC: Carson-Dellosa.

Some students will want to add more pages. Ask these students to tell you what they want you to write, and as long as they can articulate the detail, provide them with another page.

Extension: When students are comfortable with writing multipage books, present a minilesson on adding cover pages, which should include a title and the author's name. Adding "autograph pages" at the end of the book also encourages students to get a signature from everyone to whom they read the book—a great incentive for reading practice.

Making a book is a wonderful tool for the students' writing toolboxes—and many young writers will even want to make books on their own. (In this case, a minilesson on "one-click stapling" is probably in order: Put the corner of the page into the stapler, press the stapler down, and listen for one click.)

STICKY DOT DETAILS

Developmental Level: Early

Trait: Ideas

Most students do their first writing by simply labeling a picture. As they grow as writers, they need to learn to elaborate, or add more details to the topic. This minilesson uses a manipulative—sticky dots—as an incentive to add details to a topic. The dots are used to indicate the end of each detail.

Introduction: Connect this minilesson to students' understanding of topics and details. Tell them that today they will be learning about adding more than one detail to a topic.

You have become very good at choosing a topic to write about and adding a detail about the topic. But good writers usually write more than one detail about a topic. In fact, sometimes they have lots of details! For example, if my topic is "Popcorn," I might add details like, "It is my favorite snack, and it is white and fluffy like little clouds." Today, you are going to learn about writing more than one detail about a topic.

Instruction: Go through the usual process for modeled writing, but place two sticky dots on the back of your hand. Tell the students that these dots are to help you remember to write two details. Model telling what your details are before you write them.

I've got lots of ideas for topics in my head right now, but today I'm going to write about the topic "What I Did on My Summer Holidays." I know I've already used that topic, but sometimes I can use it again, if I have different ideas or more details to add. Just because you've used a topic once doesn't mean you've used it up. I'm going to use it again because this time I have a few more things to tell.

So, that's my topic—"What I Did on My Summer Holidays"—and now I need two details. My first detail is "I went camping in the mountains." My second detail is "I saw a bear."

Pretell your first detail, and then write it. Put one of your sticky dots at the end of the sentence (the detail). Then, review the second detail, write it, and place the other sticky dot at the end of that sentence. Be

sure to model rereading after every few words to keep track of your thoughts.

Application: Tell students that now it is their turn to choose a topic and write two details. Require them to pretell their two details—either to the group or to a writing partner—before they get two sticky dots on the backs of their hands. When they can pretell what they are going to write and it is clear that they understand the concept of two details, give them their writing materials to begin. Give them a few minutes for writing before you "alight" at each desk for a butterfly conference. As you visit each writer, ask him or her to read what was written. Then ask a few questions and invite the writer to tell more. If the student can add another detail, offer to give him or her one more dot.

Extension: Many students will pretell their details in complete sentences; other students will not—for example, a child who chooses a topic like "My Favorite Foods" might write a list such as "pepperoni pizza," "chocolate chip cookies," and so forth. At this point, the objective is to generate details, not write complete sentences.

In time, after the students have had practice adding several details to a topic, this is a good opportunity to make the transition from sticky dot details to writing sentences. Praise students who have written complete sentences, and invite others to see how they can turn a detail into a sentence.

How can we turn the details about "My Favorite Foods" into a sentence? Maybe "I love all kinds of pizza, but I love pepperoni the best" or "Chocolate chip cookies are my favorite dessert."

Eventually, students will replace the sticky dots with periods. (See chapter 4, "Conventions," for lessons on teaching sentences.)

FIVE-FINGER PLANNER

Developmental Levels: Early, Developing, Fluent

Traits: Ideas, Organization

The Five-Finger Planner is an organizer that can be used to help students generate several details about a topic. The organizer is in the shape of a hand, and students write the topic on the palm, one detail on each finger, and how they feel about the topic on the thumb. The organizer not only helps writers generate ideas, but it also introduces the idea of shaping a piece of writing with a concluding or "ending" sentence, which is based on how you feel about the topic.

Introduction: Connect this minilesson to previous lessons on adding details to a topic. It is a natural extension of the minilesson Sticky Dot Details.

Boys and girls, I've been noticing that you are including more and more details in your writing. Today, you're going to learn how to use a special writer's tool to help you think about several details about a topic before you write the whole piece. This tool is called a Five-Finger Planner. It's in the shape of a hand, and it's going to help you plan your writing.

Instruction: Demonstrate how to create this planner by tracing your hand on a piece of paper and modeling each step in the planning process as you think aloud (see Figure 13). You may want to have students trace each other's hands, or you can provide students with photocopies of the reproducible figure at the end of the minilesson.

On the palm of my hand drawing, I'm going to write my topic. Today, I'm going to write about the topic "My cat Cookie." On each finger, I need to write one detail about my topic. Let's see, my cat Cookie has bald eyebrows. I'll write, "has bald eyebrows" on the first finger. My cat Cookie has a skinny tail. I'll write, "has a skinny tail" on the next finger. I want to think of an idea that will surprise my reader. I know—Cookie likes to drink coffee! Isn't that funny? I'm going to write, "likes coffee" on the next finger. What else could I write? Hmmm. I could write, "My aunt has a cat, too," but that's not about my cat Cookie. I need to stick to my topic. I'll write, "jumped in the bathtub." The last thing I need to write is on the thumb of the hand, and that's how I feel about the topic. I'll write, "is a funny cat, but I love her."

FIGURE 13. Five-Finger Planner Sample

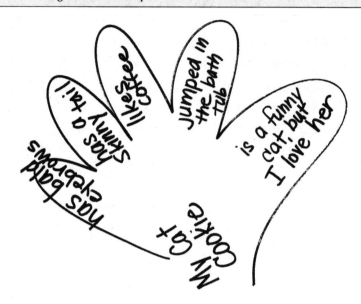

Application: Guide students through the process of completing their own Five-Finger Planners. For example, tell students to write their topics on the palm of the hand outline and ensure that they have completed this step before moving on. Then, instruct students to write one detail about their topics on each finger. Again, circulate around the classroom and guide students as they compose their details. Finally, tell students to write how they feel about the topic on the thumb of the hand.

Extension: Provide the students with several opportunities to practice completing Five-Finger Planners before turning one into a draft. Students can store the extra planners in their topic pockets. Then, follow up with the minilesson Turn It Into a Story to demonstrate how to convert the details into connected text.

Five-Finger Planner

Date

Observations

_____

_____

_____

_____

_____

_____

_____

_____

_____

Notes for Future Instruction

_____

_____

_____

_____

_____

_____

_____

_____

_____

_____

STORM AND SORT

Developmental Levels: Early, Developing, Fluent

Traits: Ideas, Organization

Storm and Sort involves brainstorming ideas on individual cards, and then sorting and sequencing them before turning them into connected text. Sometimes brainstorming alone can lead to disjointed writing, as young students tend to simply record their ideas in the same random order in which they were conceived. Although older students can organize their ideas in a web, young students seem to have more difficulty visualizing this organizational structure. By writing their ideas on individual cards, then physically manipulating them, writers are able to create a structure for their writing before they actually begin to draft it.

Although this minilesson is designated for early writers and beyond, it can be conducted with emergent writers as a shared writing activity with the teacher acting as scribe.

Introduction: Connect this lesson to previous work on generating and organizing ideas for writing.

I have noticed that you are adding more and more details to your writing. I can hardly keep up with your sticky dot details [see Sticky Dot Details, p. 57]. Some of you don't have enough fingers on your Five-Finger Planners because you have so many ideas. Today, you are going to learn how to use another writer's tool to help you think of details about your topic before you write.

Brainstorming is a word we use for thinking of lots of ideas on a topic. The writer's tool you're going to learn is called Storm and Sort because you have to brainstorm all the ideas you can on a topic, and then you're going to sort those ideas. You can sort the ideas that belong together and then think about what order you want to use.

Instruction: Use modeled or shared writing to generate ideas on a familiar topic. Large sticky notes work well with this lesson; otherwise, you can make your own cards for writing ideas.

My topic today is "Family Fun Night at School." Here are several word cards. I'm going to write one detail about Family Fun Night on each of my cards.

I went on the hayride.	It cost a quarter for three tickets.
I dunked Mr. Johnstone in the dunk tank.	I got to pet the horse.
I had pizza and chocolate milk.	I went fishing for a yo-yo.
I threw a beanbag into a dish.	I bought some candy.

Demonstrate sorting the ideas and sticking them on a large sheet of paper.

Wow, I have eight different details on my topic "Family Fun Night at School." But if I turn them into a story just the way they are, it will be a little mixed up for a reader. I know that I got to pet the horse when I went on the hayride, but my reader probably doesn't know that. So I need to put those two details together. I'm going to get a big sheet of paper and stick those two details in the same place, so I remember to write them together when I turn this into a story.

It was funny when we got to dunk Mr. Johnstone in the dunk tank! I'm going to put all the details about the games I played in another spot.

Complete the demonstration by sorting all of the details and pasting them on the large sheet (see Figure 14).

Application: Now have the students complete their own Storm and Sort exercise. You may want to have students work in pairs on a shared topic the first time they engage in this activity. By working with a partner, students can extend their ability to brainstorm details and their discussion helps consolidate their understanding.

Extension: After the students have had several opportunities to practice Storm and Sort, conduct a minilesson on how to turn the plan into connected text, as in the minilesson Turn It Into a Story.

Date

Observations

Notes for Future Instruction

FIGURE 14. Storm and Sort Sample

Family Fun Night

What I did

I got to pet the horse.

I went on the hayride.

Games

It cost a quarter for three tickets.

I threw a bean bag into a dish.

I dunked Mr. Johnstone in the dunk tank.

I went fishing for a yoyo.

What I ate

I had pizza and chocolate milk.

I bought some candy.

3-2-1 PLANNER

Developmental Levels: Early (as a shared writing activity), Developing (with support), and Fluent

Traits: Ideas, Organization

The 3-2-1 Planner is a graphic organizer that represents *three* key ideas, *two* details for each idea, all on *one* topic. This graphic organizer helps writers organize a piece of writing into three parts, usually beginning, middle, and end, and then plan supporting details for each part. It helps writers ensure that all the key information is in place and unrelated details are omitted. This tool lends itself to narrative writing (personal and fictional narratives) but also is adaptable to informational writing.

Introduction: Connect this minilesson to students' experiences with generating many ideas on a topic.

Now that you are writing lots and lots of details on a topic, sometimes there are details that don't belong or that aren't quite in the right place. Before you draft a piece of writing, it is helpful to plan which main ideas and details you are going to include.

Today, you are going to learn how to use a special kind of planner called a 3-2-1 Planner to help you plan and organize your big ideas and details. 3-2-1 stands for <u>three</u> key ideas, <u>two</u> details for each, all on <u>one</u> topic.

Instruction: Use the 3-2-1 Planner at the end of the minilesson to model your own story plan.

Here's how to use the 3-2-1 Planner. I start with my topic in the first box. Then in the three boxes below, I write what happens at the beginning, in the middle, and at the end of the story.

THE DAY THE RAFT SANK

Julie and I snuck down to the slough and got on our raft.	The raft sank in the middle of the pond and we jumped off.	We hung our jeans in the tree house and sat in our underwear to wait for them to dry.

That's a pretty good start, kind of like the skeleton of my story. Now I'd better add some details to each of those key ideas. [Think aloud as you model completing the organizer. See Figure 15.]

Date

Observations

Notes for Future Instruction

NOTES

Date

_____

Observations

_____
_____
_____
_____
_____
_____
_____
_____

Notes for Future Instruction

_____
_____
_____
_____
_____
_____
_____
_____
_____
_____
_____
_____
_____
_____
_____
_____

FIGURE 15. 3-2-1 Sample

The Day the Raft Sank

Julie and I snuck down to the slough and got on the raft.

> A slough is a dirty old pond where cows drink.

> We were 10 years old and not allowed to go rafting on the slough.

The raft sank and we jumped off.

> the raft was an old waterlogged door

> slough wasn't too deep but our jeans were soaking wet.

We hung our jeans in the tree house and sat in our underwear to wait for them to dry.

> cold fall day

> "shivering in our skivvies"

With this completed planner, now I can write my story without missing any important details or adding details that don't fit.

Application: Photocopy the 3-2-1 Planner, and provide each student with a copy to complete. Have students select a topic from their Writing Ideas Bingo cards to plan a piece of personal writing. (You may want to present this as a guided writing lesson and walk the students through each step of the process.)

Extension: The 3-2-1 Planner may be adapted to a variety of different forms of writing. For example, students can use the planner to prepare for informational writing, as shown in the following:

SNAILS

Body		Habits		Interesting Facts	
Fact 1:	Fact 2:	Fact 1:	Fact 2:	Fact 1:	Fact 2:
• have eyes on the end of their feelers	• carry their shell on their back	• move by making mucus for sliding	• breathe through a hole in their shell	• its body is called a foot	• leave a trail of mucus

3-2-1 Planner

Topic or starting sentence					
Beginning		Middle		End	
Detail	Detail	Detail	Detail	Detail	Detail

TURN IT INTO A STORY

Developmental Levels: Early, Developing, Fluent

Traits: Ideas, Organization, Conventions

This minilesson helps you model for students how to convert the notes from a prewriting organizer to connected text. Although the lesson modeled here follows the Five-Finger Planner, it may be conducted as a follow-up to any prewriting plan. Several writing elements are modeled in this lesson, including combining similar details, editing out repeated words, and writing a concluding statement.

Introduction: Connect this minilesson to students' previous work on the Five-Finger Planner. Show students how you choose one of your Five-Finger Planners and "turn it into a story" (see Figure 16).

We have been working for a few days on Five-Finger Planners. A planner is simply a list of details about a topic. Today, you are going to learn

---

FIGURE 16. Turn It Into a Story Sample

My cat Cookie has bald eyebrows and a skinny tail. She likes coffee. One day she jumped in the bath tub. I think Cookie is a funny cat.

---

how to take the details from one of your Five-Finger Planners and turn it into a story. I think I've got some pretty interesting details on this planner about my cat Cookie, so I'm going to work with this one.

Instruction: Review each of the details on your planner and think aloud as you convert the details to connected text.

> My cat Cookie has bald eyebrows. My cat Cookie has a skinny tail.

I think I could combine those two details into one sentence because they're both about how Cookie looks. So I need to remember to use the word <u>and</u>.

> My cat Cookie has bald eyebrows and a skinny tail.

That's the end of that sentence, so I put a period there.

Now I want to put in the next detail, "my cat Cookie likes coffee." But I have to be careful about saying "my cat Cookie" too many times. It gets boring for a reader if I say the same thing over and over and over. So instead of "my cat Cookie" I think I'll say, "She likes to drink coffee." I'm just going to add that right on to the first detail. It's a new sentence, so I'll start with a capital letter and put a period at the end. I need to remember to leave a space between my lines in case I need to add something later.

> My cat Cookie has bald eyebrows and a skinny tail. She likes to drink coffee.

My next detail is "My cat Cookie jumped in the bathtub once." I think I'll say "she" again instead of "my cat Cookie." You know what, I think I'll start my sentence with "One day." And I'll just add that right on.

> My cat Cookie has bald eyebrows and a skinny tail. She likes to drink coffee. One day, she jumped in the bathtub.

And now I'm going to end with how I feel about Cookie. Remember on your Five-Finger Planner, you wrote about how you feel about the topic on the thumb of the hand.

> My cat Cookie has bald eyebrows and a skinny tail. She likes to drink coffee. One day, she jumped in the bathtub. I think Cookie is a funny cat.

Application: Now provide the opportunity for students to select one of their Five-Finger Planners to turn into a piece of writing. You may want to review the important items students will need to remember when they write.

NOTES

Date

Observations

Notes for Future Instruction

Date

Observations

Notes for Future Instruction

You have a lot of things to remember when you turn your Five-Finger Planner into a story:

First, think about which detail you want to put first and next and so on. Second, you might want to combine two details into one sentence if they go together. Third, if you prefer not to, you don't have to put the details in the same order that you have them in on your Five-Finger Planner. Fourth, remember that it's not interesting for readers if you repeat the same words over and over, so think about using different beginnings for your sentences. Fifth, each new sentence needs to begin with a capital letter and end with a period. And finally, make sure to leave a space between each line in case you want to add something later.

As the students are writing, circulate among them to offer guidance and support.

CHAPTER 3

Substance and Style:
The Writer's Craft

THE SECOND-GRADE CLASS that wrote the collaborative poem on "hugs" featured in Figure 17 knew some things about writing. They knew that good writing has a rhythm and a flow. They knew that good writers choose their words carefully and play with language to create "surprising" images in the reader's mind. In other words, they knew something about writer's craft.

Writer's craft is a phrase that refers to style or "polish" in writing. Writer's craft goes beyond *what* the writer says to *how* he or she says it, and includes elements like effective word choice, personality, style, and rhythmical language. Author Mem Fox (1993) says, "*craft* is understanding the nature

FIGURE 17. Writer's Craft Sample

Hugs

Diapers hug babies.
Envelopes hug letters.
Bandages hug boo-boos.

Icing hugs cupcakes.
Spots hug a giraffe.
Stars hug the sky.

and importance of leads and endings; of structure and focus; of showing, not telling; of purpose and audience.... *Craft* means being able to put those understandings into practice" (p. 20).

The minilessons in this chapter focus on helping writers develop their craft by addressing topics such as sensory images, engaging leads, satisfying conclusions, powerful words, and interesting dialogue (see Table 11).

When children first begin to think about writing as "talk written down," they record whatever words come to mind. They may use incorrect words ("remote-*patrol* car"), write phonetic spellings of mispronounced words ("My *bruzzer's* name is Jamie"), or inadvertently use figurative language to represent ideas that they don't have names for ("When I was sleeping I saw pictures in my pillow"). Oral language facility is an important precursor to well-crafted writing; a child's repertoire of words will either impede or empower his or her writing. At this time in their lives, most children have a limited number of words they can read, but they have access to a much wider range of words for writing. Any word they can say, they can write. That's one reason why it is critical to teach students to use phonetic or "invented" spelling; it ensures that students are not restricted to the words they know how to spell conventionally. (See chapter 4, "Conventions," for more information on invented spelling.)

As emergent writers progress to early and developing levels, they begin to attend to the words they use rather than just using whatever words come to mind. They start to use modifiers; for example, instead of writing, "I was hot," they might write, "I was *really* hot." By the time they reach the fluent writing stage, students are able to make deliberate and effective use of language. In fact, one of the defining characteristics of fluent *readers* is their ability to understand and interpret figurative language, the language of books (Rog, 2003). For this reason, it's important to help students at all stages of development build a repertoire of vivid verbs, precise nouns, and marvelous modifiers to enhance both their print and verbal communication.

Powerful writing is a work of art. The words are the palette and the writer's voice the strokes of the brush. Consequently, three minilessons in this chapter support young writers in painting pictures with words. **Painting Word Pictures** scaffolds students as they revise a piece of patterned writing to add more depth and description. This minilesson uses a guided writing approach, in which the teacher demonstrates, facilitates, guides, and supports students while allowing them to practice what they have learned (Routman, 1994). Although there are many different models of guided writing, the one used in this minilesson involves guiding writers through the composition and revision of a piece of text. This lesson includes the use of a

TABLE 11. Writer's Craft Minilessons at a Glance

Lesson Name	What It Teaches	Developmental Level	Trait	Pages
Painting Word Pictures	Descriptive writing and revising	Emergent Early Developing Fluent	Ideas Word choice Sentence fluency	76–79
Show, Don't Tell	Descriptive writing	Developing Fluent	Ideas Word choice	80–81
Five-Senses Descriptions	Multisensory descriptions	Emergent Early Developing Fluent	Ideas Word choice	82–84
Hook the Reader	Effective leads	Developing Fluent	Organization Voice	85–87
Wrap-Around Endings	Satisfying conclusions	Developing Fluent Adaptable to emergent and early	Organization	88–92
Traffic-Light Words	Transitions	Early Developing Fluent	Organization	93–95
Linking Words	Conjunctions	Developing Fluent	Sentence fluency	96–98
Stretching Sentences	Building sentences	Early Developing Fluent	Ideas Word choice Sentence fluency Conventions	99–102
Add Some Talking	Dialogue	Developing Fluent	Ideas Voice Word choice	103–105
Notice It, Name It, Try It	Literary techniques	Developing Fluent	Voice Word choice Sentence fluency	106–108

pattern poem adapted from the theme book *Halloween* (McCracken & McCracken, 1988).

Show, Don't Tell has been described as "the first rule of writing" (McClanahan, 2000). This minilesson teaches students to use specific details to tell a story. **Five-Senses Descriptions** reinforces the concept of "showing, not telling" by teaching students to use sensory images in a descriptive piece about food.

As previously mentioned in chapter 1, a sense of audience is critical knowledge for a writer (Graves, 1983). Teaching students to think about the reader on the other end of their writing helps them write with more passion, clarity, and personality. When writers think about their audience, they consider things like how to create writing that will grab the reader's attention, enable the reader to follow the text with ease, and leave the reader feeling satisfied with a neat resolution. **Hook the Reader** models one of several "super ways" to start a piece of writing. **Wrap-Around Endings** offers a simple formula for writing conclusions, based on actual leads and conclusions from classroom literature (Rog & Kropp, 2004).

Writer's craft entails not only the *style* of the text but also the *sound* of the text. Effective writing flows smoothly and rhythmically. Transition words serve to "link... sentences and paragraphs together smoothly so that there are no abrupt jumps or breaks between ideas" (Owl Online Writing Lab, Purdue University, ¶ 1). **Traffic-Light Words** teaches students about important transition words that act as "bridges" between ideas to enable the reader to seamlessly cross from one idea to another. Research from the Qualifications and Curriculum Authority (1998) reports that frequent use of transition words is an indicator of longer sentences and more sophisticated writing.

One important way to create rhythmical writing is to have students vary the lengths of their sentences, beginnings, and structures (Culham, 2005). Sentence combining is one of the most useful grammatical activities for improving writing (Hillocks, 1986). In the minilesson **Linking Words**, students who are stuck in the writing mode of short, choppy sentences will learn to use conjunctions and prepositions to combine sentences. **Stretching Sentences** is a dynamic, interactive lesson that shows writers how to take a core sentence and extend it with modifiers and prepositional phrases.

The trait of voice—personality, flair, style, or whatever label educators choose for it—is the trait that makes a piece of writing speak to a reader (Culham, 2005). Voice is that elusive element in a piece of writing that evokes laughter, sadness, peacefulness, anger, indignation, or warmth. Ironically, beginning writers often start writing with plenty of voice. But sometimes, as students focus more and more on conventions and correctness, their writing becomes stilted. One technique for enhancing voice in a piece of writing is inserting dialogue, as demonstrated in **Add Some Talking**.

Many experts have written about the value of the reading–writing connection (Routman, 2005). Teaching our students to "read as writers" helps them learn the techniques writers use. In our classroom read-alouds, we need to read each book first as a reader, then as a writer. The power of rereading familiar text has been well supported in reading research (National Institute of Child Health and Human Development [NICHD], 2000). Calkins (2003) uses the term "author mentors" to refer to books that teach children about writer's craft. Fletcher and Portalupi (2001) remind us that "writing without reading is like seesawing alone.... We need to tap [children's] experiences as readers if we really want them to soar" (p. 84).

The last minilesson in this chapter, **Notice It, Name It, Try It**, is a unique approach to helping students construct their own understandings about writers' techniques. When the students "notice" writing techniques, figurative language, and literary devices in their reading, they can record it. Having the students "name" these techniques helps them consolidate the learning and create a label that is meaningful to them (Calkins, 2003). (Teachers may choose to teach students the "official" names of particular techniques, when appropriate.) Finally, students take the opportunity to "try it," and practice the technique in a safe and scaffolded setting. Ultimately, we want students to add each technique to their own writing toolboxes, so they are better able to add style and strength to their independent writing.

Writer's craft is what turns mundane writing into text that will engage readers and evoke emotional reactions. Can the youngest writers write with craft? Can developing writers balance emerging competence with style and charm? For some students, writer's craft will come naturally; for most students, it will emerge and become refined as a result of having strong models, experiencing explicit teaching, and having opportunities for practice and immersion in the context of authentic writing tasks. The minilessons in this chapter are intended to enhance these learning experiences for young writers.

PAINTING WORD PICTURES

Developmental Levels: Emergent, Early, Developing, Fluent

Traits: Ideas, Word Choice, Sentence Fluency

Painting Word Pictures is a series of three minilessons that employ a writing framework based on the days of the week. Through these lessons, students are guided through writing and revising a free-verse poem over several days. Each day, the teacher models an exercise for composing and revising the text, and then the students engage in the same process with their individual pieces. Painting Word Pictures is a good exercise for reinforcing revision techniques because it requires students to add, insert, and replace words. Because the students are given a framework, they don't have to worry about the text structure and are able to focus on choosing words that "paint pictures" in the reader's mind.

Painting Word Pictures is useful for writers at all stages of development, but the number or "layers" of revisions will depend on the sophistication of the writers. Because the students are scaffolded in their writing, they are able to demonstrate greater sophistication than they would be capable of on their own.

Introduction: Talk to the students about how writers use words to help readers visualize what is happening in the text. Connect this concept to examples in student writing:

I just love it when you use "wow" words in your writing to paint pictures in a reader's mind. When Joshua said, "I was so scared my hair spiked," I could picture his hair in my mind. When Cassidy said, "I wiggled and jiggled and danced all around," I had a wonderful picture of her movements.

Today, you're going to practice painting word pictures by writing a poem about spring. I'm going to give you part of the poem. You just have to finish each line with a word picture.

Instruction and Application: In this series of minilessons, instruction and application are integrated as you guide students through composing and revising the poem. It reinforces the revision processes of adding on details and pushing words described in chapter 5.

Day 1
Prepare a copy of the poem framework (found at the end of the minilesson) on a sheet of chart paper or overhead transparency.

Boys and girls, I'd like you to close your eyes for a minute and make a picture in your mind about what you see in the spring. Please help me finish each line in the poem with a word that is something you see in the spring.

Invite the students to contribute appropriate nouns to complete each line of the common text. Three lines of text (i.e., Monday, Tuesday, Wednesday) are adequate for the shared writing example, because it is only intended to teach the concepts and processes of revising the text to create word pictures. For example, your poem might read as follows:

I knew it was spring because
On Monday, I saw one <u>rainbow</u>.
On Tuesday, I saw two <u>robins</u>.
On Wednesday, I saw three <u>tulips</u>.
And that's how I knew it was spring.

Then, cover or remove the shared writing piece, and provide the students with their own individual copies of the poem framework. Instruct students to complete their own pattern poems. If they include some of the ideas you used, don't be concerned. Many students will not have the necessary vocabulary yet to create their own ideas. Preparing a theme bank of "spring words" ahead of time will help provide your students with a repertoire of words from which to draw.

Day 2
Revisit the same poem and revise it by adding on details at the end of each line.

Boys and girls, we started some nice poems yesterday about spring. But a good poem should use words that paint a picture in the reader's mind. Look at our first line, <u>On Monday, I saw one rainbow</u>. Take a picture of that rainbow in your mind. What was it doing?

Use this process to complete each line with a verb and a "where," "when," or "how." The revised poem might read as follows:

I knew it was spring because
On Monday, I saw one rainbow <u>shining in the sky</u>.
On Tuesday, I saw two robins <u>chirping messages to each other</u>.
On Wednesday, I saw three tulips <u>waving in the breeze</u>.
And that's how I knew it was spring.

Again, cover your copy of the poem, and invite the students to return to their poems and add a verb phrase to each line. Tell students to think about the "spring things" they wrote about, and add on a word or words to tell what they were doing, when or where they did it, or how they did it in order to paint a better word picture of that object.

Day 3
Revisit the same poem again to model inserting adjectives and other descriptors.

Boys and girls, I am so excited about the poems we've been writing for the past two days. You have been using some great action words and I can just picture your spring ideas in my mind. Today, we're going to see if we can add to those word pictures by adding describing words. Let's read the first line together: <u>On Monday, I saw one rainbow shining in the sky</u>. Hmm, what kind of rainbow was that? I think it was a colorful rainbow. So I'm going to "push in" that word <u>colorful</u> right before the word <u>rainbow</u>. Now, would you help me think of some more describing words for the rest of the lines?

Read each line chorally and brainstorm adjectives for each noun. If several words are offered, try them out by reading the line and then vote on which one the students think sounds best and paints the best word picture.

I knew it was spring because

      colorful
On Monday, I saw one ^ rainbow shining in the sky.

      busy
On Tuesday, I saw two ^ robins chirping messages to each other.

    delicate   spring
On Wednesday, I saw three ^ tulips waving in the ^ breeze.
And that's how I knew it was spring.

Again, cover the collaborative poem and invite students to revisit their own poems to add descriptors.

Extension: Have students select their "best" lines from their poems. Go around the room in "round-robin" style and invite each student to read aloud his or her best line. Encourage students to listen for "wow" words to borrow for their own writing.

Use this framework for a variety of themes (e.g., the ocean, Halloween, the farm, trip to museum, and so forth).

I Knew It Was Spring

I knew it was spring because

On Monday, I saw one _____

_____

On Tuesday, I saw two _____

_____

On Wednesday, I saw three _____

_____

On Thursday, I saw four _____

_____

On Friday, I saw five _____

_____

And that's how I knew it was spring.

SHOW, DON'T TELL

Developmental Levels: Developing, Fluent

Traits: Ideas, Word Choice

Teachers often say to students, "Show, don't tell," when they want students to use descriptive details in their writing. Rather than *telling* the reader, "He was cold," we want to *show* the reader, "His teeth chattered and his lips turned blue." This minilesson uses a guided writing approach to help make the concept of *showing* more explicit and to provide students with practice in revising their writing.

Introduction: Here is an opportunity to show your dramatic flair. Storm into the classroom with a furious expression on your face, and shake your head and wave your arms. Shout or mutter something such as "I can't believe it" or "This isn't fair." Then, revert to your normal sweet, gentle persona (and if necessary, tell students you were just acting), and ask students how they think you were feeling when you came into the classroom. Unless you're a truly dismal actor, they should be able to determine that you were angry. Ask students how they knew you were angry, and record their responses on a chart:

- Your face was red and had an angry expression.
- Your eyes were squinted.
- You were shaking your arms in the air.
- You were shouting.

If I had come into the room and said to you in a normal, quiet voice, "I am so angry," would you have believed me? Instead of telling you that I was angry, I showed you. That's what good writers do: Instead of telling us things, they show us. Today, you're going to learn about showing.

Instruction: Show students a student writing sample such as the one that follows.

Ms. J marched into the classroom with a stormy look on her face. She waved her arms and shouted, "You won't believe what just happened." Someone had just run into her car in the school parking lot.

The writer of this piece didn't need to tell us that she was angry. Instead she showed us, using words like <u>a stormy look on her face</u> and <u>waved her</u>

arms and shouted. Using "show, don't tell" is another way to paint a picture in the reader's mind. For example, if we wanted to describe the terrible storm last week, what could we say?

With the students, brainstorm descriptions of a storm such as the following:

- The wind was blowing leaves and branches off the trees.
- The icy rain felt like little slivers hitting my face.
- Flashes of lightning lit up the whole sky.

Then, create a shared text with the brainstormed ideas. Your text might read as follows:

When we came out of the school, the wind was blowing so hard that it pushed me along the slippery sidewalk. The icy rain felt like little slivers hitting my face. I could hardly see across the street. I thought I would never get home that day.

Application: Have students practice the "show, don't tell" technique in pairs. Give each pair of students a "telling" statement and have them generate (orally or in writing) two descriptions that "show."

Some "telling statements" for practice might include the following:

- He was rich.
- She was cold.
- My room is a mess.
- She's/He's such a good friend.
- The garden was beautiful.
- I felt very sad.

FIVE-SENSES DESCRIPTIONS

Developmental Levels: Emergent (orally), Early, Developing, Fluent

Traits: Ideas, Word Choice

This guided writing lesson introduces students to writing descriptions using their senses—sight, smell, taste, sound, and touch. It is a good follow-up to Show, Don't Tell because it gives writers some additional tools for description.

Writing about food is a good way to introduce young writers to multisensory descriptive writing because it focuses on many of the senses. This lesson uses "zebra cookies," chocolate wafers with vanilla cream filling.

For emergent writers, conduct the lesson orally as a shared writing activity. For early writers, it may be helpful to provide a framework such as the Five-Senses Framework at the end of the minilesson. Developing and fluent writers should organize the details on their own.

Introduction: Connect this lesson to work the students are already doing with descriptions. Find a sample text or a previous modeled-writing lesson to use as an example. Remind students that description can involve more than just what something looks like, and tell them that they will be learning about how to describe something using all of their senses.

I'd like to share a wonderful piece that Jordie wrote last week about his favorite food, spaghetti and meatballs:

> I love spaghetti and meatballs! They look like worms and eyeballs! But they are yummy in my tummy!

I love the way Jordie gave us a surprising detail about how his spaghetti and meatballs "look like worms and eyeballs." That's kind of yucky, but it paints a picture in my mind! First, Jordie told us how his spaghetti and meatballs look, and then he told us how they tasted. Jordie is using his senses to describe his favorite food. Today, you are going to learn about using all of your senses to describe your favorite food.

Instruction: Prepare a chart such as the Five-Senses Framework to record students' ideas. Give each student a zebra cookie, and tell students not to eat the cookie until you tell them to do so. Have the students look carefully at the cookie and turn it on all sides so they can describe what it looks like. Encourage them to use "just like" words such as "black and white just like a penguin" or "striped just like a zebra." As the students offer their ideas, record their words on the chart. Then tell the students to smell the cookie and describe the smell. Follow this by asking the students to take a bite and tell how it feels in their mouth, how it sounds when they chew it, and finally how it tastes. You may want to make some suggestions to stimulate more figurative language such as, "It feels like _____ in my mouth," or "What are some other words like *crunch* to describe how it sounds?"

Application: After you have recorded all the sensory descriptions, invite students to choose the descriptions they like best to use in a "zebra-cookie description."

Boys and girls, from now on, I want you to think about zebra-cookie descriptions whenever you are writing. These descriptions will help you remember to use smell, taste, sound, and touch words and "just like" words when you write.

Words related to colors, numbers, and emotions (e.g., anger, sadness) extend children's imaginations as well as their vocabulary base.

Extension: Repeat this minilesson with different topics—topics other than food. Not all senses will work with every topic, but it reminds students to think about sensory descriptions in addition to appearance. Draw attention to literature examples of sensory descriptions such as the book *Owen* (Henkes, 1993), which describes how Owen's blanket "Fuzzy" looks, smells, tastes, and feels.

Date

Observations

Notes for Future Instruction

Five-Senses Framework

My zebra cookie looks like _____.

It smells like _____.

When I put it in my mouth, it feels like _____.

When I chew on it, it sounds like _____.

When I swallow it, it tastes like _____.

My zebra cookie is _____.

HOOK THE READER

Developmental Levels: Developing, Fluent

Traits: Organization, Voice

In a piece of writing, an effective lead has to "hook" the reader's attention, so he or she wants to continue reading. This minilesson models a technique for starting a piece of writing in a way that "hooks" the reader.

Additional ways to start a piece of writing are described in the Extension section of this lesson. Each technique should be taught separately, in the context of a piece of modeled writing or a student example. As you discuss different ways to begin a piece of writing, add examples to the classroom chart (see Figure 18) for students' ongoing reference.

FIGURE 18. Classroom Chart of Effective Leads

Super Ways to Start

1. **Start by making the reader wonder**
   unusual, funny, strange, interesting
   mysterious

2. **Start by asking a question**

3. **Start with some talking**

4. **Start with a PUNCH**
   Oh no!   Not again!   At last

5. **Start with a fact**

6. **Start with an opinion**

7. **Start with the weather**

NOTES

Date

_____

Observations

_____
_____
_____
_____
_____
_____
_____
_____

Notes for Future Instruction

_____
_____
_____
_____
_____
_____
_____
_____
_____
_____
_____
_____

Introduction: Connect this lesson to what the students know about creating texts with a beginning, middle, and end.

Writers, you've been working really hard to organize your writing so it has a beginning, middle, and end. Today, we're just going to think about the beginning, the very first sentence in a piece of writing. You know, I think the first sentence might very well be the most important sentence in the whole piece. The first sentence is called the "lead" because it leads the way to the rest of the piece. The job of the lead is to "hook" the reader's attention and make the reader want to read more. Today, you're going to learn how to create leads that "hook" the reader's attention.

Instruction: Show students several "literary mentors," or models from literature, of effective leads that provide just enough information to make the reader wonder what will come next. Some examples include the following:

- "There's a silly old saying that if you hold a guinea pig up by its tail, its eyes will drop out." (*I Love Guinea Pigs*, King-Smith [2001])
- "It all started with one little string of tiny white Christmas lights." (*The Amazing Christmas Extravaganza*, Shannon [1995])
- "That's it," said Miss Bugscuffle. "Permanent Lifelong Detention...unless you have one very good and very believable excuse." (*Baloney, Henry P.*, Scieszka [2001])

Discuss with the students which leads "hook" their attention and why.

All of these authors thought very carefully about their lead sentences because they wanted to hook our attention. And they all made us wonder and want to read more. I wonder if a guinea pig's eyes really will drop out? Maybe the book will tell me. I wonder what all started with the string of Christmas lights? And I wonder what that person has done to get "Permanent Lifelong Detention"?

Today, you're going to learn how to write lead sentences that hook a reader's attention so he or she will want to read on to see what the rest of the piece says.

Revisit some previous writing models that you used in class so you can model how to add engaging leads.

Remember this piece I wrote about my cat Cookie? I can go back and revise it—or make it better.

My cat Cookie has bald eyebrows and a skinny tail. She likes to drink coffee. One day, she jumped in the bathtub. I think Cookie is a funny cat.

You know what I'm missing? A lead sentence to hook the reader's attention. I think I'm going to write, "My cat Cookie is a very unusual cat." Words like <u>unusual</u> often make a reader wonder—what's so unusual about her—and want to read on to find out.

Create a classroom chart of "Super Ways to Start a Piece of Writing" and add "Make the reader wonder," along with an example from literature or from the modeled writing. You may want to include a list of words that "make the reader wonder," such as *unusual, interesting, amazing, surprising,* or *strange.*

Choose two or three more examples of previous modeled-writing texts. Brainstorm with students and generate "hooks" that could make the reader wonder.

Application: Tell students that sometimes writers plan the lead sentence ahead of time and sometimes they don't know what the lead is going to be until *after* they've finished the piece of writing. Invite students to start a new piece of writing with a lead that "hooks the reader" or to find a previous piece of writing to which they could add a new "hook."

Extension: Over time, provide students with a repertoire of different ways to start a piece of writing. Maintain a reference chart with various techniques for writing "hooks." For example, based on the suggestions on the classroom chart in Figure 18, my writing model could be adapted as follows:

- Start by making the reader wonder—My cat Cookie is a very unusual cat.
- Start by asking the reader a question—Have you ever seen a cat drink coffee?
- Start with some talking (dialogue)—"Here, kitty, kitty. Come have your bath."
- Start with a punch—Oh no! Not again!
- Start with an interesting fact—My cat thinks she's a person.
- Start with an opinion—I think cats are just like people.
- Start with the weather—It was pouring rain the day that Cookie got lost.

Date

_____

Observations

_____
_____
_____
_____
_____
_____
_____
_____

Notes for Future Instruction

_____
_____
_____
_____
_____
_____
_____
_____
_____
_____
_____
_____

WRAP-AROUND ENDINGS

Developmental Levels: Developing, Fluent, Adaptable to Emergent and Early

Trait: Organization

A common but effective way to end a piece of writing is to revisit the beginning. This minilesson uses a game format with literary mentors to show young writers how they can pull a few key words from the lead sentence to create an effective concluding sentence that "wraps around" the piece of writing.

The "Beginnings and Endings Game" incorporates leads and conclusions from various children's picture books. Some samples are provided at the end of the minilesson.

Introduction: Connect this lesson to previous discussions on beginnings and endings. For example, the concept of ending with how you feel about a topic was introduced in Turn It Into a Story (p. 68).

You have been working a lot on writing leads that hook the reader's attention. Good endings also are important. A good ending is like the bow on a present—it wraps up the piece neatly. You've learned how to end a piece of writing with how you feel about the topic. Today, you are going to learn another technique for ending a piece of writing—the "wrap-around" ending.

Instruction: Prepare for the game by printing all the leads on green strips of paper and all the conclusions on blue strips of paper. Give each student one sentence strip with a lead (green) or a conclusion (blue). Then, instruct students to find their "partners"—that is, the person with the other colored strip from the same story. Explain to students that when they have found their partner, they should stand together and hold their strips in the air until everyone has found a partner. You may want to provide students with one model of a beginning–ending connection to ensure the students understand what they are supposed to do.

After everyone has found his or her partner, invite each pair to share their beginning and ending with the class. Post a few of the examples on a classroom chart to revisit later. Then use the activity to discuss the common technique that each author used.

Isn't it amazing that you could match all these beginnings and endings without reading the whole book? That's because all of these books have "wrap-around" endings. The ending just "wraps around" to the beginning! Let's look at what Eve Bunting did in Night Tree [1991]. She took those two key words Christmas and tree and made a wrap-around sentence.

Look at some of the other examples and talk about what key words the author used from the lead sentence to make an ending sentence.

Wrap-around sentences are a technique that writers use to finish off a piece of writing neatly. You just pick two or three important words from the lead sentence and use them in the ending sentence to add the "bow on the present."

Follow up by working with students to create wrap-around endings for some of your previous modeled-writing texts or other student examples such as "The Monster":

The Monster

Last night I had a bad dream. It was a scary monster. He was so hairy that you could not see his eyes. He tried to jump on me. I woke up. It was my cat. He was purring and lying down on me.

Ask students to determine what important words to pull from the opening sentence to put in the wrap-around sentence. Students also can work in pairs to come up with an ending sentence such as "It wasn't a bad dream after all!" or "I'm glad I woke up from that dream."

Application: Choose some modeled-writing samples from previous lessons to practice writing wrap-around sentences as a group. Then invite students to find a writing piece in their writing folders for which they can create a new wrap-around ending.

Extension: Send students on a "treasure hunt" for wrap-around endings in literature. Visit the picture book section of the school resource center and turn them loose with instructions to come back with one book in which the ending sentence revisits the beginning sentence. Have students share their findings with the class.

The "Beginnings and Endings Game" may be adapted for emergent and early writers by reading aloud a lead sentence, and then reading

Observations

Notes for Future Instruction

two or three alternative ending sentences. Have the students listen to the choices and choose the ending that they think goes with the beginning that you read. Remember that students should have opportunities to talk about the elements of effective writing even before they are able to demonstrate them.

Some examples that work well with this game (and are referenced in the samples provided) include the following:

- *The Table Where Rich People Sit* (Baylor, 1994)
- *Night Tree* (Bunting, 1991)
- *Click, Clack, Moo: Cows That Type* (Cronin, 2000)
- *Rotten Ralph* (Gantos, 1980)
- *Chrysanthemum* (Henkes, 1996)
- *Hooway for Wodney Wat* (Lester, 2002)
- *If You Give a Pig a Pancake* (Numeroff, 1998)
- *The First Thing That Mama Told Me* (Swanson, 2002)

Sentence Strips for the Beginnings and Endings Game

Beginnings

On the night before Christmas, we always go to find our tree.

The day she was born was the happiest day in her parents' lives. She was absolutely perfect.

Ralph is Sarah's rotten cat, but Sarah loves him anyway.

If you give a pig a pancake, she'll want some maple syrup to go with it.

Poor Wodney. Wodney Wat.
His real name was Rodney Rat, but he couldn't pronounce his *r*'s.

Farmer Brown has a problem. His cows like to type. All day long he hears "click, clack, moo, clickety clack, moo."

If you could see us sitting here at our old scratched-up homemade kitchen table, you'd know that we aren't rich.

When I was born, the first thing my mama told me was my name.

(continued)

Sentence Strips for the Beginnings and Endings Game (continued)

Endings

Chrysanthemum did not *think* her name was absolutely perfect. She *knew* it!
And they're all there together, singing their own Christmas songs on Christmas Day around our tree.
"Hooway for Wodney Wat!" they cried. "Woot! Woot! Wooty-toot-toot!"
Ralph decided never to be rotten again...except for sometimes when Mother cooked lobster for dinner.
The next morning he got a note: "Dear Farmer Brown, The pond is quite boring. We'd like a diving board. Sincerely, The Ducks." Clickety clack quack.
I think the title of my book is going to be "The Table Where Rich People Sat."
Then my name went flying out into the big, starlit night.

TRAFFIC-LIGHT WORDS

Developmental Levels: Early, Developing, Fluent

Trait: Organization

Transition words are an important tool for organizing writing, but they can be a challenge for writers of all ages. This minilesson uses an analogy to green, yellow, and red traffic lights to teach students about different types of transitions.

Introduction: A basic way to introduce students to transitions is to use a procedural writing sample. For example, I start with a previous modeled writing lesson using the sample "How to Blow Out Birthday Candles."

When we wrote this piece "How to Blow Out Birthday Candles," we used numbers to tell what order the steps followed. But we can use words instead of numbers to show order, too. Today, you're going to learn about special kinds of words that are like bridges from one idea to another.

Instruction: Together, reread the shared writing piece "How to Blow Out Birthday Candles."

> *Do you want to know how to get your birthday wish? Here's what you have to do:*
> *1. Make a wish.*
> *2. Take a deep breath.*
> *3. Blow out all the candles on your cake.*
> *I hope you will get your birthday wish.*

Then, together, suggest words that could replace the numbers 1, 2, and 3 in the piece.

I think I'm going to put the word <u>First</u> beside "Make a wish," instead of the number 1.

Invite the students to suggest words that could replace numbers 2 and 3. "Push in" an appropriate transition word for each.

> *Do you want to know how to get your birthday wish? Here's what you have to do:*
> *First*
>   *^ make a wish.*

Next
° take a deep breath.

Last
° blow out all the candles on your cake.
I hope you will get your birthday wish.

Prepare a chart with three columns and label the columns with "Green-Light Words," "Yellow-Light Words," and "Red-Light Words," or photocopy and enlarge the chart at the end of the minilesson. Tell the students to think about what they know about traffic lights.

Writers, just think for a minute about traffic lights. When you're in the car with your mom or dad and the light turns green, the change in color tells her or him to start going. The yellow light means you can keep going, but you need to be careful. And we all know that the red light means stop. Words can act the same way: They tell readers to start, keep going, or we're almost at the end.

I thought that we could trade the word <u>first</u> for the number 1. I think <u>first</u> is a pretty good green-light word. Can you think of any more?

Complete the chart with as many words as the students can come up with. Keep the chart on display as a reference that students can add to when they discover new transition words.

Application: Have students work independently or with a partner to write a new three-step "how-to" piece using a green-light word, a yellow-light word, and a red-light word. To reinforce the concept, students can circle the green-light word with a green marker, the yellow-light word with a yellow marker, and the red-light word with a red marker.

Have students look at the writing in their portfolios to find traffic-light words they already used. Again, students can circle them with an appropriately colored marker. Encourage students to look for places in existing writing where they can "push in" a traffic-light word.

Extension: Remind students to be on the lookout for traffic-light words in their reading. For example, if you read a book such as *Meanwhile, Back at the Ranch* (Noble, 1992), you could add the word *meanwhile* to the class chart.

Traffic-Light Words

Green-Light Words	Yellow-Light Words	Red-Light Words

LINKING WORDS

Developmental Levels: Developing, Fluent

Trait: Sentence Fluency

This lesson teaches students to use conjunctions to create compound sentences. It is a good lesson to use when you notice students using a lot of short, choppy sentences, typical of many developing writers. Later, the lesson may be extended by adding subordinate conjunctions (e.g., *when, after, if*) to create complex sentences. A gesture of linking forefingers or a visual model of paper links can help reinforce the concept of linking words.

Introduction: Connect this lesson to other minilessons and practice students have been doing with writing sentences. (See chapter 4, which deals with conventions.)

I've noticed that you are paying very careful attention to writing good sentences with a "who" or "what" part and a "does" or "is" part. You are careful to put capital letters at the beginning and periods at the end, just as I have in my new story, "My Dog Maxi."

> Maxi thinks she's a person. She doesn't like dog food. She likes ice cream. She watches TV. She barks at the phone. What a crazy dog!

Let's count how many sentences I have here. [Frame the sentences as the students count them.] Now let's count the words in my sentences. Oh, no, they all have four or five words! No wonder my writing sounds a little bit choppy. Sometimes when sentences are all the same length, the writing sounds choppy to read.

Today, you're going to learn how to use linking words to join up short little sentences to make some longer ones. When writing has some short sentences and some longer ones, it sounds smoother when we read it.

Instruction: Use the sample writing piece above or find or create your own sample with a number of short, choppy sentences.

I'm thinking about which sentences to join. I think "Maxi thinks she's a person" will hook the reader's attention, so I'm going to leave it by itself. But the next two sentences, "She doesn't like dog food" and "She likes ice cream," could go together because they're both about what Maxi eats. I could join those two sentences with the word <u>but</u>. [Use a caret to insert the word <u>but</u>.] Let's see how it sounds: "She doesn't like dog food but she likes ice cream." Let's put the word <u>but</u> on a chart that we'll call our "Linking Words" chart (see Figure 19).

Now let's take a look at the rest of the piece. I think I would like to join the next two sentences, "She watches TV" and "She barks at the phone," because they're both about what she does. Can anyone help me with a word? [Invite students to contribute words and try them out.] "She watches TV <u>but</u> she barks at the phone." Maybe that could work. "She watches TV <u>and</u> she answers the phone." I think the word that sounds right and makes sense here would be <u>and</u>. Let's read it together: "She watches TV <u>and</u> she barks at the phone."

As you read other people's writing, listen for the words they use to join sentences. When we learn other linking words, we will add them to our chart so we can use them in our own writing.

Application: Encourage students to look for places in an existing writing piece where they may "push in" a linking word to join two short sentences, or provide a writing sample for students to work on together to join sentences.

In your writing today, I would like you to find ways to join sentences with a linking word. You might go back into a piece of writing you have

FIGURE 19. Linking Words Chart

already finished to push in a linking word or you may use a linking word as you draft new sentences. When I come to your desk, show me a place where you have used a linking word. Did anyone notice that I just used the linking word <u>when</u>? We use linking words all the time.

Extension: Maintain a reference chart (such as the one shown in Figure 19) with linking words that you and the students encounter in your reading and writing.

STRETCHING SENTENCES

Developmental Levels: Early, Developing, Fluent

Traits: Ideas, Word Choice, Sentence Fluency, Conventions

This engaging and interactive minilesson is intended to help students understand the process of constructing and crafting complex sentences. It not only addresses writer's craft—ideas, word choice, and sentence fluency—but also reinforces grammar and sentence structure.

For this minilesson, students hold word cards at the front of the classroom as they stretch the sentence with additional words or phrases. The students contribute the necessary words and phrases, and the teacher acts as the scribe. As an extension of this activity, students exchange words in the sentences then "shrink" the sentence by deleting unnecessary words.

Students need to have a foundational understanding of simple sentences ("who" or "what" and "is" or "does") before they start working on sentence stretching. This interactive exercise helps to extend what students know about basic sentences and guides them in crafting more complex sentences.

Introduction: Draw on students' knowledge of basic sentences.

Writers, we have been talking a lot about groups of words called sentences. You'll remember that a sentence needs two parts: a name part (who or what) and a doing part (is or does). Today we're going to play the sentence-stretching game to help you learn how to take a sentence and stretch it out by adding words that tell when, where, and what kind.

Instruction: Start with a simple sentence. You may want to use one of the students' ideas or provide a starter yourself, such as the following example:

The children played.

Print each word on a separate word card in print large enough for everyone to see. Have three students hold up the word cards to create a sentence. Invite the other students to add ideas to stretch the sentence. (The first few times this lesson is conducted, you will need to provide some guidance on what kinds of words we can use to stretch

Date

Observations

Notes for Future Instruction

the sentence, but later the students will be able to generate ideas on their own.)

Be sure to provide a period on a sticky note because it may have to be moved as the sentence is stretched. Using capital letters on sticky notes also reinforce students' understanding of conventions. For example, when a word is added to the beginning of the sentence, the capital letter on the previous word must be removed.

Invite the students to contribute by responding to the following question: "What did the children play?" Add a suggestion to an individual card and send a student to the front of the classroom to hold the card. Then ask: "Where did they play? When did they play?" Each time, add appropriate words; for example, groups of words such as *after school* or *on the playground* could be written as a complete phrase on the word card. Invite students to discuss where to place added words or phrases. Should *after school* go at the beginning of the sentence or at the end? Have the student holding the card move to the front of the sentence and to the end and read it both ways for students to judge which arrangement sounds better. (You may need to have a vote.) The final sentence might read as follows:

After school, the noisy children played tag on the playground.

Application: Students may need some guidance in writing their own "stretched-out" sentences. The graphic organizer at the end of the minilesson may be used for practice. As you confer with students, you might point out sentences here and there and ask, "How could you stretch that sentence?" or "Can you show me a stretched-out sentence in your writing today?" Remind them that they can stretch out a sentence by adding when, where, why, what kind, or how, but they always must have the basic two parts: who or what and is or does.

Students will be at various stages in their ability to write extended sentences on their own, but this oral sentence-stretching activity will go far to help build understanding of sentence variety and fluency.

Extension: When students have grasped the idea of "stretching" sentences, extend the activity by having students "trade" words in the sentence. For example, students might trade the word *teachers* for *children* or the phrase *in the park* for *on the playground*. (The key here is that the sentences are syntactically correct, not logical or sensible. Students take great delight in creating sentences like, "After school, the silly teachers played tag in the hallway.")

Other variations of this activity include "shrinking" the sentence. ("What words could we take away and still have a correct sentence?") After stretching and trading, the new "shrunken" sentence is often completely different from the original one.

The graphic organizer also may be used as a shared or independent writing activity. When it is completed, cut apart the squares to make new "silly sentences."

Date

Observations

Notes for Future Instruction

Sentence Stretching Graphic Organizer

What Kind?	Who or What?	Did What?	Where?	When?	Why?
funny	clowns	danced	around the ring	while the ringmaster was talking	to make everyone laugh

ADD SOME TALKING

Developmental Levels: Developing, Fluent

Traits: Ideas, Voice, Word Choice

Good writers know that dialogue adds voice and interest to a piece of writing. This minilesson focuses on inserting dialogue for effect.

Introduction: Connect this lesson to previous classroom discussions about making a piece of writing more interesting for a reader to read.

Boys and girls, you are getting very good at writing stories with details and with a beginning, middle, and end. But good writing also needs to tell the story in a way that will be interesting for the reader. Today, you're going to learn how to add some talking to a piece of writing to make it more interesting to read. When someone talks in a piece of writing, writers call it "dialogue."

Instruction: Use a piece of student writing to demonstrate how to add dialogue such as the following example.

It's my birthday today. I woke up my mom and dad but they said it's too early. I went down to the kitchen. I saw a birthday cake. I was happy that I got a cake. Then Mom and Dad woke up. I opened my presents.

This is one student's story about his birthday. You know, I think if I wrote this story, I'd sound a lot more excited than this writer does. One way that I can add some personality and voice to this piece of writing is to "push in" some talking—what writers call "dialogue."

Let's pretend it's your birthday and you wake up really, really early, all excited about opening your presents. You go into your mom and dad's bedroom, but they're still sound asleep. What are you going to say?

Ask students to suggest dialogue; most likely, they will come up with something like, "Wake up, Mom and Dad." Then, invite one student to act out the scene with you as the parent. The dialogue will probably sound something like the following:

Child: Wake up, Mom.

Parent: It's four o'clock in the morning. Go back to bed.

Date

_____

_____

Observations

_____

_____

_____

_____

_____

_____

_____

_____

_____

Notes for Future Instruction

_____

_____

_____

_____

_____

_____

_____

_____

_____

_____

_____

_____

Remind students that in writing, you have to tell who is doing the talking. Think about the way each sentence was expressed and generate appropriate tag lines that identify who the speaker is and in what way he or she is speaking.

Would you say, "Wake up, Mom" in a normal voice? Would you whisper? If you're excited and you want them to hear you, you would probably yell, "Wake up, Mom and Dad!" in great big capital letters with one of these excitement marks (exclamation marks). So now the sentence would read:

"Wake up, Mom and Dad!" I yelled.

On a subsequent revisiting of this minilesson, you might talk about putting the tag line before or after the dialogue and choosing which arrangement sounds better to the writer.

Now, what kind of voice do you hear me answer in? Maybe we should add, <u>Mom groaned</u>.

Mom groaned, "It's four o'clock in the morning. Go back to bed."

After reviewing the dialogue orally, model inserting it into the text. (It may be necessary to "stretch the paper," as modeled in chapter 5). As you write, remind students that dialogue needs a tag line and quotation marks.

Writers, there are two things we need to do to show talking in our writing: One is to add the words <u>he yelled</u> or <u>she said</u> or <u>Mom groaned</u>. The other is to use talking marks [gesture with your fingers] around just what the person said.

It's my birthday today. "Wake up, Mom and Dad!" I yelled. "It's four o'clock in the morning," Mom groaned. "Go back to bed." I woke up my mom and dad but they said it's too early. I went down to the kitchen. I saw a birthday cake. I was happy that I got a cake. Then Mom and Dad woke up. I opened my presents.

Ask the students questions such as, What do you suppose the writer might have said to his mom and dad? What do you think they said back to him?

Application: Encourage your students to find an existing piece of their own writing into which they can insert dialogue, or provide them with a piece of writing.

Not all of your students will be at a place where they can add dialogue to an existing piece of writing, but be sure to draw attention to it when a student does use some dialogue and encourage "adding some talking" when conferring with students.

Date

Observations

Notes for Future Instruction

NOTICE IT, NAME IT, TRY IT

Developmental Levels: Developing, Fluent

Traits: Voice, Word Choice, Sentence Fluency

This minilesson uses children's books to introduce literary techniques to students. When students notice a writing technique in a children's book, they give it a name and then try it in their own writing. Naming the technique is a powerful exercise because when students name it, they feel as if they "own" it. And when they understand a particular technique, they are more likely to apply it to their own writing. These ideas are all recorded on the "Notice It, Name It, Try It" chart (see Figure 20).

Introduction: Connect this lesson to a shared experience with a piece of literature that uses interesting language or techniques.

Sometimes when we read books together, we notice words the writer has used that stick in our mind. When we were reading <u>Saving Sweetness</u> [Stanley, 1996] the other day, you all laughed at words the writer used, like "nasty enough to scare night into day" or "I'm gonna knock you into the middle of next week." The writer, Diane Stanley, thought about all the words she used to make the book interesting for us as readers. Today, you're going to learn about how you can use some of those special ways that writers put words together.

Instruction: As you read the book aloud a second time, pause regularly to talk with the students about what words and expressions they notice. At the end of the reading, guide the students in selecting one of the expressions they noticed to put on the "Notice It, Name It, Try It" chart.

Writers, you've decided that you want to put the phrase "nasty enough to scare night into day" on the "Notice It, Name It, Try It" chart. I agree that it is a very clever way to put words together. It certainly does make us realize how mean and scary Ms. Sump was! [Record the phrase on the chart.]

Instead of "nasty enough," what if we said, "kind enough to..."? How could we finish off that phrase? [Invite student suggestions, e.g., "Kind enough to make the sun shine on a cloudy day."] What if I said she was "angry enough to..."? "Smart enough to..."? Or we could say, "The sun was hot enough to..." or "The diamond was shiny enough to...."

FIGURE 20. Notice It, Name It, Try It Chart

Techniques Writers Use

Notice it! Name it! Try it!

"the high, soft shusshh-whine of the runners" (Dog Team) — Sound words — "pptt-pptt-pptt" went the popcorn

"nasty enough to scare night into day" (Saving Sweetness) — enough to... — bright enough to turn my eyeballs backward in my head!

"as sad as a shrimp" (Quick as a Cricket) — "just like" words — as slippery as jello

"my sister Sophie is super-completely and totally THE. MESSIEST" — LOUD writing — We were SNOWED IN!

Date
_____

Observations
_____
_____
_____
_____
_____
_____
_____
_____
_____

Notes for Future Instruction
_____
_____
_____
_____
_____
_____
_____
_____

Brainstorm responses to variations of this expression. Then guide the students to think of a name for this writing technique.

Shola has suggested that we call this technique "enough to..." writing. Diane Stanley said "nasty enough to...," and we could say "hot enough to..." or "funny enough to..." in our own writing.

When the students have agreed on a name for the technique, record it on the chart and generate a few examples together. The name that students choose is not as important as its connection to their shared understanding and application of the technique. This moment is a good opportunity to engage in some class writing; as mentioned in chapter 1,

students can "hitchhike" from one another to brainstorm creative examples of "enough to..." writing.

Application: Tell students that they now can add the "enough to..." technique to their own writing toolboxes to make comparisons when describing how smart someone is or how heavy something is. When you confer with students, point out opportunities where they might insert the "enough to..." technique.

Extension: Repeat this minilesson as needed. "Enough to..." writing is only one of many techniques students will encounter in their literary mentors. Sometimes you may want to tell the students the "official" name for a technique, such as alliteration, after they have generated their own name (such as "same-sound words"). However, the value of this strategy is empowering students to construct their own meaning for the technique.

Many picture books apply wonderful language and sophisticated literary techniques. Some examples include the following:

- *Things That Are Most in the World* (Barrett, 2001)
- *Hoops!* (Burleigh, 1997)
- *Twilight Comes Twice* (Fletcher, 1997)
- *Feathers and Fools* (Fox, 1996)
- *Achoo! Bang! Crash! A Noisy Alphabet* (MacDonald, 2003)
- *Dogteam* (Paulsen, 1993)
- *Quiet as a Cricket* (Wood, 1990)

CHAPTER 4

Conventions: The Nuts and Bolts of Writing

WHEN I WAS in first grade, astronaut John Glenn became the first American to orbit the earth. After a short class discussion, the teacher gave each of us a piece of writing paper and told us to write about this momentous current event. Gripping my oversized pencil, carefully printing between the "grass" and the "sky" lines on the page, I began: "On Feb. 20, 1962, John Glenn...." So far, so good. I could copy that much from the chalkboard. Now I wanted to print that wonderful word *orbited*. "Or...ar...oar...," I sounded out. After several struggles and much erasing, I gave up and wrote, "went around the earth."

In 1962, writing was all about correct spelling and grammar, even in first grade. If you didn't know how to spell a word, you just didn't use it. Today, over 40 years later, we struggle to find a balance between encouraging students to choose the most powerful words and setting standards for correctness. After all, writers write for readers and if the writing is not readable, even the most unique idea, most clever thought, or most powerful wording is lost. Through much of history, there was little consistency in the way English words were spelled. Gradually, a set of common standards, or "conventions," were established to enable one person to read another person's writing, which is why we refer to spelling and grammar as "conventions" of writing. The minilessons in this chapter focus on teaching concepts about spelling, capitalization, punctuation, and other grammatical constructs (see Table 12 for an overview of the minilessons).

One of the first conventions that young writers learn is "word boundaries," the concept that individual words have spaces around them. When young children begin to write, they string ideas together without attention to separating words. "Concept of word" is the ability to match the spoken word to the written word. The idea of words as separate entities is unfamiliar; after all, we don't speak in individual words, we speak in streams of words. But, as Morris (1993) suggests, the development of this understanding is critical to developing a sight-word vocabulary and may also facilitate phonemic awareness. Finger tracking and "framing," or cupping words with the hands and isolating words with word framers, are techniques many teachers use to reinforce "word boundaries" in reading. A trip to the local dollar store can yield creative and inexpensive manipulatives for isolating words, such as toy magnifying glasses, plastic fly swatters with "word holes" cut into the center, or assorted items to be used as pointers. **Count the Words** is a minilesson that helps reinforce voice to print matching by having students chant the words and the spaces as they count on their

TABLE 12. The Nuts and Bolts of Writing Minilessons at a Glance

Lesson Name	What It Teaches	Developmental Level	Trait	Pages
Count the Words	Concept of word	Early	Conventions	115–116
Bubble Gum Writing	Invented spelling	Early Developing	Conventions	117–119
Borrowing Words From the Wall	High-frequency words	Emergent Early Developing Fluent	Conventions	120–121
Tricks for the Tricky Parts	Memory tricks to help students spell words	Early Developing Fluent	Conventions	122–124
Shortcut Words	Contractions	Early Developing Fluent	Conventions	125–128
Capital-Letter Word Sort	Proper and common nouns	Early Developing Fluent	Conventions	129–131
Silly Stories	Different structures and types of words	Early Developing Fluent	Word Choice Conventions	132–135
Name Part and Doing Part Sentences	Building sentences	Early Developing Fluent	Conventions	136–137
Talking Marks	Punctuating dialogue	Developing Fluent	Conventions	138–140
Be Your Own Editor	Editing for conventions	Early Developing Fluent	Conventions	141–144

fingers before writing. Ultimately, we want students to remember to put "spaghetti spaces" between the letters and "meatball spaces" between the words.

Most children go through fairly predictable stages as they progress from scribbling to conventional spelling and grammar (Bear, Invernizzi, Templeton, & Johnston, 2000). As they learn the shapes and sounds of the letters in the alphabet, they begin to experiment with using those symbols to represent words. Temporary, phonetic, or invented spelling, regardless of what we choose to call it, is one of the most important tools we can give our students for writing. Many researchers have documented the value of invented spelling as a tool for helping young writers develop language concepts, for supporting decoding, and for scaffolding conventional spelling (Dahl & Freppon, 1995; Richgels, 1995; Wilde, 1997). This process of "educated guessing" about how a word is spelled enables young writers to construct knowledge about how language goes together. Phonetic spelling requires writers to apply their knowledge of sounds and patterns of language to construct words. It promotes writing fluency and enables young writers to access any word in their speaking vocabulary. Clarke (1988) found that first-grade children who were encouraged to use invented spelling not only used a greater variety of words than their peers who did not use invented spelling but they also scored higher on tests of both spelling and word recognition. Burns, Griffin, and Snow (1999) assert that "when children use invented spelling, they are in fact exercising their growing knowledge of phonemes, the letters of the alphabet, and their confidence in the alphabetic principle" (p. 102). The minilesson on **Bubble Gum Writing** teaches students to stretch out a word to hear all of its component sounds, and then represent each sound they hear with a letter.

Some of our students will be reluctant to write any word they don't know how to spell conventionally and thereby limit the range of vocabulary they can access for writing. Thus, it's important for us to demonstrate, reinforce, and praise the use of invented spelling. Ray and Cleaveland (2004) keep a class chart called "I'm Not Afraid of My Words," on which they celebrate examples of "fearless spelling." Some teachers refuse to help with the spelling of words, preferring that students use their own problem-solving skills. I help students with spelling, but only after they have tried the words themselves first. This establishes an expectation that the students will try the word and move on. When I am available to help, their invented spelling enables me to celebrate what they know and offer quick, explicit instruction on a strategy for spelling that word the next time.

Although we want our students to continue spelling phonetically as needed, we also expect them to build an increasing repertoire of conventionally spelled words. Even at the earliest stages of writing development, there are certain words that are so common to writing that we want students to recognize and spell them quickly and automatically. Fewer than 100 words make up over half the reading and writing we do (Fry, Kress, & Fountoukidis, 2000). (No wonder we call them "high-frequency" words.) These words are the "glue" words that holds writing together, so it is important that student writers be able to spell these words automatically. Unfortunately, most high-frequency words—such as *of, does, the,* and *to*— do not follow predictable spelling patterns. Therefore, these words must be carefully taught and reinforced using a variety of learning modes.

The word wall is an important tool for teaching high-frequency words (Cunningham & Allington, 1998). A word wall is more than a display of words; it is a tool for explicit teaching and reinforcement. A small number of words is introduced each week—then spelled, cheered, chanted, written, compared, and posted on the wall. Once a word is on the wall, it is a "no-excuse" word and must be spelled correctly at all times. Although our goal is for students to be able to spell these words independently and automatically, the word wall remains visible as an ongoing reference for students. We can't assume, however, that students will automatically be able to make the transfer from the wall to the paper. **Borrowing Words From the Wall** provides a quick, multisensory routine for helping students use the word wall as an ongoing resource for spelling high-frequency words.

As we establish expectations for our students to spell more and more words conventionally, we want to give them tools and strategies for remembering the conventional spellings of words. **Tricks for the Tricky Parts** teaches students to create memory tricks or *mnemonics* to help them remember the "hard parts" of the words they frequently spell.

There are many different kinds of words in the English language. Instruction in grammar and syntax helps young writers sort out when to use a plural or singular noun, or when they should use an apostrophe. **Shortcut Words** teaches students how to create contractions, and **Capital-Letter Word Sort** focuses on proper and common nouns. To pull it all together, **Silly Stories** is a variation of a popular party game that requires students to generate different kinds of words and then insert them into a prewritten story.

The "word sort" (Bear et al., 2000; Gillet & Kita, 1979) may be used to teach a host of language concepts and grammatical constructions. Word sorting is an activity that requires students to categorize words based on a particular criterion that may be defined by the teacher (i.e., a "closed" sort) or left for students to discover based on similarities and differences in the words (i.e., an "open" sort). Words may be sorted according to beginning sounds, letter patterns (such as rimes or consonant blends), or morphological chunks (such as prefixes or root words). This activity has many strengths: It requires students to actively engage with words, to conceptualize and make decisions about the patterns and differences among words, to articulate and communicate their thinking, and to look at words in unique ways to construct their own generalizations about language concepts.

When our students demonstrate the ability to write groups of words, they can begin organizing those words in sentences. For many of our students, seeing and hearing correct models of sentences do much to establish "sentence sense." Routman (2005) asserts that "students learn about sentences and paragraphs not by studying about them in isolation, but through reading widely, hearing good literature, reading aloud and writing for audiences and purposes that matter" (p. 154). But some teachers prefer to supplement that incidental instruction with explicit instruction in constructing and revising sentences. Unfortunately, sometimes we confuse our students by telling them that a sentence is a "complete thought" or a sentence "makes sense." The reality is that we have plenty of complete thoughts that are not complete sentences: "Where are you going?" "Home." "When?" "Right now." "By yourself?" "With my brother." Each of the bits of thought is quite complete for the speakers—and even for us as readers. But they are not complete sentences. A more explicit definition of a sentence is a special group of words that has a *who* or *what* and an *is* or *does*, a definition that is presented in **Name Part and Doing Part Sentences.**

Of course, sentence work also requires conventional use of punctuation. Students need to understand that punctuation is more than just little marks on a page; it can change the voice, tone, and even the meaning of a piece of writing. Consider the following example: "Woman without her man is nothing." Punctuated as "Woman, without her man, is nothing," the line carries quite a different message than "Woman—without her, man is nothing." Students need to understand the forms of punctuation as well as the functions they perform in a sentence in order to help the reader create the same meaning that the writer intended. A minilesson on **Talking Marks** focuses on helping students create and punctuate dialogue in their writing. (This lesson may be effectively linked with Add Some Talking, p. 103.)

When our students have a good repertoire of conventionally spelled words, know how to use capital letters and punctuation, and have some sense of sentence structure, they are ready to start editing their own writing. Cunningham and colleagues (2005) state that teaching editing is "the only proven way to teach children writing rules they actually use when they write" (p. 62). Furthermore, when students are expected to edit their work, they are more inclined to take more care with initial drafts. For most students, this occurs at the end of the early writing stage, usually around the middle of first grade. **Be Your Own Editor** consolidates all of the learning on conventions as students are taught to start taking responsibility for their own editing.

Teaching students to edit their own writing means that we as teachers need to give up that responsibility. Although there are times when we will want to serve as "editor-in-chief" before a piece of student writing goes public, most writing should be edited by the writer him- or herself before it is published. Students learn very quickly that they don't need to take responsibility for correct conventions if we always do the work for them.

Teachers walk a fine line between setting standards for correctness and encouraging our students to take risks in their writing. Even in second and third grades, the more complex the sentences our students write, the more likely they will be to make grammatical errors. The more sophisticated the words they choose, the more likely they will be to make spelling errors. Obviously our expectations for conventions will vary with the needs of the students. We need to assess our students' writing to see what they are ready to learn in order to make decisions about what to teach them. There is no point in teaching sentences if our students are not yet writing words. There is no point in teaching quotation marks if our students are not ready to use dialogue in their writing.

Conventions, perhaps more than any other writing trait, vary a great deal by stage of writing development. As Spandel (2003) says, keep your expectations realistic. Focus not on perfection but on growth.

Conventions exist for the purpose of enabling someone else to read our writing. If we didn't have writing, we wouldn't need conventions. Therefore, we must teach conventions in the context of writing and ensure that our students have opportunities to apply what they have learned to their own writing. By providing explicit teaching, sensitive scaffolding, and high expectations, we help our student writers create writing that reflects both appropriate conventions and powerful craft.

COUNT THE WORDS

Developmental Level: Early

Trait: Conventions

The concept of "word boundaries" is a difficult one for many young students. Speech usually does not help students to distinguish individual words because it sounds like a stream of sounds. Therefore, we need to help students hear and write words as separate entities. This lesson uses finger counting to reinforce word boundaries.

Introduction: Connect this lesson to what students already know about words—their names are a good place to start.

We know that writing is putting our talk down on paper. When we talk, we use lots of words at a time. When we write, we just write one word at a time and put a space between each word. Today, you're going to learn a trick for counting words by using your fingers.

Instruction: This minilesson is effectively presented in the context of shared or interactive writing, especially working with the texts the students compose collaboratively. Figure 21 shows an example of interactive writing.

Boys and girls, the other day we talked about having a cookie sale to raise money for Project Love [a charity that purchases school supplies for children in developing countries]. Today, we're going to write a note to Mr. Johnstone, our principal, to ask him if it's okay for us to have a cookie sale. How should we get started?

Have the students say the words together, "Dear Mr. Johnstone," and show them how to count the words on their fingers: Hold up your right hand, and as you say each word, point to one finger. Be sure to say the word *space* between each word and point to the space between each finger as you say it.

Dear—space—Mr.—space—Johnstone—space.

Start with the baby finger and bend down the forefinger, as a reminder of when to stop counting. Count how many fingers you touched—in this case three.

FIGURE 21. Interactive Writing Sample

cook
cookie
look
book

ear
Dear
fear
hear

s a l e

? ?

DD

Dear   Mr.   Johnstone,
May   we   have   a
Cookie   Sale   for
Project   Love ?
From   Grade 1

Now we know that "Dear—Mr.—Johnstone" is three words and three spaces.

As you (or a student) write the phrase on chart paper, have one student act as the "spacer" by putting his or her hand between each word.

Invite the students to compose the next sentence—for example, "May we have a cookie sale for Project Love?" This time students will need to count the fingers on two hands.

Model and practice this exercise as you complete the text.

Application: After the students have practiced counting words in the shared or interactive writing lesson, remind them that they should count words *before* they write their own sentences.

Before you write, it's important to whisper to yourself the words you're going to use and count them on your fingers, so you have all the spaces you need. Then, when you write, remember to put spaghetti spaces between the letters and meatball spaces between the words.

BUBBLE GUM WRITING

Developmental Levels: Early, Developing

Trait: Conventions

"Stretching out" a word to hear all the sounds (i.e., phonemic awareness) and representing every sound with a letter (i.e., phonics) are the basic tools of using sound strategies for invented spelling. The National Reading Panel (NICHD, 2000) reported that phonemic awareness is effectively taught in conjunction with letter work. In addition, teaching phonemic awareness helps lay the groundwork for temporary (invented, phonetic) spelling, which helps develop conventional spelling concepts (Clay, 1991). The purpose of this lesson is to teach young writers to segment words and represent each constituent sound with an appropriate alphabet letter. This lesson asks students to think of a word as a piece of bubble gum that can be "stretched" out of the mouth with one hand as they listen for the sounds and then write them with the other hand.

Introduction: Connect this minilesson to students' experience with writing words they don't know how to write in conventional or "book writing."

When you write, you use lots of different words. Sometimes you already know how to write a word in book writing, or you can find it on the word wall, or you know another place you can find it in book writing. But when you don't know how to write a word in book writing, there's something else you can do: bubble gum writing. Just pretend the word is a piece of bubble gum in your mouth and s-t-r-e-t-c-h it out as you listen for all the sounds. Today, you're going to learn how to do bubble gum writing with any kind of word.

Instruction: Demonstrate "bubble gum writing" in the context of a modeled writing lesson. Explain why you are using bubble gum writing and how you are doing it.

I am going to show you how I can use bubble gum words in my writing. If I know the "book writing" of a word, I will use it. But I may not know the book writing of a word I want to write. That's when I can stretch out the word like a piece of bubble gum so I can hear all the sounds in it, and then I write a letter for every sound I hear.

Date

Observations

Notes for Future Instruction

Date

_____

_____

Observations

_____

_____

_____

_____

_____

_____

_____

_____

_____

Notes for Future Instruction

_____

_____

_____

_____

_____

_____

_____

_____

_____

_____

_____

_____

_____

The topic I'm going to write about today is how cold it is outside. Here is my picture of us having indoor recess. I am going to write two details: "It is cold outside" and "We have to stay inside for recess."

Here's how I start: I know how to write those little words <u>it</u> and <u>is</u> in book writing because we learned them for the word wall. Now I need to write <u>cold</u>. I'll put that word <u>cold</u> in my mouth like a piece of bubble gum and stretch it out: ccccc-oooo-llll-dddd. Now for each new sound that I say, I'm going to write a letter that goes with that sound. /c/ could be a <u>c</u> or a <u>k</u>, but I'm going to guess a <u>c</u> because it starts just like <u>Corey</u> on our name wall. /o/ is easy—it's that letter <u>o</u> saying its name. /l/ is <u>l</u> like in my name, <u>Lori</u>. And /d/ is <u>d</u>. Listen—as I say all those letters together quickly, they sound like /cold/.

Next, I need to write the word <u>outside</u>. Everyone put that word in your mouth and stretch it with me. Look at your partner and see the shape his or her mouth makes, just like an <u>o</u>. I'll write <u>o</u> and <u>t</u>, then I can start <u>side</u>: sssss-iiii-dddd. To finish the word, I'll put <u>ot</u> and <u>sid</u> together to spell <u>otsid</u>.

At the end of this lesson, I have a writing model that says, "It is cold otsid. We have to sta insid for reses" (see Figure 22). (In most circumstances, I use conventional spelling for modeled writing, unless I am specifically demonstrating bubble gum writing.) And, although the focus of my lesson is representing each sound with a letter, I can still provide incidental modeling of other concepts such as spaces around words and syllabication.

FIGURE 22. Bubble Gum Writing

It is cold otsid. We have to sta insid for reses.

Application: Have students practice writing a few words in bubble gum writing. Remind students that your bubble gum writing might look a little different from someone else's. The important thing is that you can read it yourself.

Now I know that every one of you knows how to do bubble gum writing. And today, during writing workshop, I'm going to ask you to show me the words you wrote using bubble gum writing.

After writing, during sharing time, draw students' attention to some of the words they wrote during writing workshop, and celebrate both their experimentation and their proximity to conventional spelling.

Extension: Ensure that students understand that invented spelling is valued and expected in the writing workshop. If they know how to write a word in book writing, they should use it; if they don't know the word in book writing, they should use bubble gum writing. Support this expectation by not helping students spell a word unless they have tried it independently first.

Assessing students' use of bubble gum writing can provide valuable information about their phonetic skills and guide planning for instruction in letter patterns and "no excuse" words.

Date

Observations

Notes for Future Instruction

BORROWING WORDS FROM THE WALL

Developmental Levels: Emergent, Early, Developing, Fluent

Trait: Conventions

The high-frequency word wall is an important resource for young writers (Cunningham, 1995). Words that have been systematically taught and mounted on the word wall should be "no-excuse" words; in other words, they should be spelled correctly every time they are written, no matter what the context is. However, many students may be unable to make the transfer from seeing a word on the word wall to writing it on their papers. This minilesson offers a multisensory (i.e., visual, auditory, kinesthetic) process for retaining word wall words for immediate use in writing.

Introduction: Connect this lesson to students' knowledge of using the word wall as a resource for writing. Tell them that they are going to learn a trick for "borrowing" a word from the word wall.

Sometimes we need to "borrow" a word from the word wall to help us remember how it is spelled. Today, you're going to learn a special trick for looking at a word wall word so you will be able to remember it and write it on your paper.

Instruction: The following process helps students use sight, sound, and movement to transfer a word from the word wall to their papers. As students develop facility with the process, it should become quick and automatic.

Prepare a chart describing the steps below for the students to reference, when necessary (see Figure 23), and then discuss the steps in detail.

1. Say the letters softly to yourself and listen to your voice.
2. Say the letters softly to yourself and trace them on your desk.
3. Say the letters softly to yourself and take a picture of the whole word in your mind.

Present this routine in the context of a modeled writing lesson so students see how it is used as a tool for writing.

I am writing an invitation to my friend to have lunch at my house. I

FIGURE 23. Steps for Borrowing Words From the Wall

Say the letters to yourself and...

 1. Hear the letters.

 2. Trace the letters.

 3. Take a picture of the word.

want to double-check the spelling of the word <u>have</u> that I know is on the word wall. I know the first letter is <u>h</u> so I look under the letter <u>h</u> to find the word. Now that I've found it, I say the letters to myself quickly three times. The first time, I say the letters <u>h-a-v-e</u> and listen to my voice. The second time, as I say the letters, I'm going to trace each one on my desk. The third time, as I say the letters <u>h-a-v-e</u>, I'm going to close my eyes and take a picture of the whole word in my mind. Now I'm going to print the word on my paper, using my memory of the sound of the letters, the way I traced it on my desk, and the picture of the word in my mind.

Application: Together with the students, practice following the three-step process for printing a few words in isolation. Remind students to use this process during writing whenever they are unsure of the spelling of a word wall word.

TRICKS FOR THE TRICKY PARTS

Developmental Levels: Early, Developing, Fluent

Trait: Conventions

One way to help students make transitions between temporary and conventional spelling is to teach students to identify the "hard parts" of words and come up with their own techniques, or "tricks," to remember how to spell them. This minilesson may be used as part of a word-wall activity or as part of a modeled writing lesson.

Introduction: Introduce the lesson by reminding students of the difference between bubble gum writing (i.e., temporary spelling) and book writing (i.e., conventional spelling). Tell students that this lesson is intended to help them think of "tricks" to aid them in remembering the hard parts of words in book writing.

Boys and girls, I've been noticing that you are writing a lot more words in book writing. Remember that book writing is the kind of writing that everyone can read and everyone spells the same way. We write all of our word-wall words in book writing. For example, that word <u>for</u> on the word wall is always spelled <u>f-o-r</u> in book writing. When you write a word, have you noticed that usually some parts of the word are easy to remember and some parts are harder? Today, you're going to learn how to remember more words in book writing by thinking about the tricky parts.

Instruction: Model for the students a process of identifying the "tricky part" of a common word and creating a "trick" for remembering it.

When we spell a word in book writing, some parts of the word are easy to remember and some parts are hard to remember. The funny thing is that sometimes the hard parts are different for different writers. What's hard for me may not be hard for you. The part that's hard for you may be easy for me. Let's look at this word <u>they</u> [write it out] on the word wall. Sometimes I want to write it as <u>thay</u> [write it out] because that's how it sounds to me. I've noticed that some of you have trouble with that word, too. It's easy for me to remember that <u>they</u> begins with <u>th</u> and ends with <u>y</u>. It's that vowel in the middle that's the "hard part," because <u>e</u> doesn't usually make an /ay/ sound. So I made up a little trick to help me remember it. My trick is to tell myself that <u>they</u> has the little word <u>the</u> in it.

We can use little tricks like this any time we want to spell a hard word in book writing. First, we look for the "hard part," then we make up a trick to remember it. Here's another tricky word from our word wall: _said_. Sometimes I notice people wanting to write _sed_ because that's how it sounds. What's the tricky part? [Invite students to respond.] Talk to your neighbor for a minute about what you might tell yourself to help remember the tricky part. [Give students time to discuss and come up with their own clues. Write them all down on a chart and review them. Add your own, if you wish.] My trick is to think of the phrase "I said I was sad," so I remember that _said_ is spelled _sad_ with an _i_ in the middle. Choose the trick that will work best for you to remember _said_ and write it on your own chart.

Application: Photocopy and distribute to each student the "Tricks for the Tricky Parts" chart at the end of the minilesson. Have students work in pairs to choose three words from the word wall that have tricky parts for them, and come up with a "trick" for each. Students should record their tricks on their individual charts and store them in their writing folders.

When students make errors in common words in their writing, have them record the words on their "Tricks" charts.

Date

Observations

Notes for Future Instruction

Tricks for the Tricky Parts

Word	"Tricky Part"	My Trick to Remember It
they	*e*	Write the word *the* and add *y*

SHORTCUT WORDS

Developmental Levels: Early, Developing, Fluent

Trait: Conventions

This minilesson helps students draw an analogy between contractions and shortcuts. Students create shortcuts with words—that is, they manipulate letter tiles to remove letters from words and replace them with apostrophes.

Introduction: Ask students to think about the concept of taking a shortcut when they are going somewhere. Then make the link between shortcuts and contractions—contractions are like shortcuts because some of the letters have been removed from their longer versions and because they are quicker to say and to write.

Boys and girls, sometimes when I'm going to the corner store from the school, I walk down Queen Street for two blocks, then I make a right turn on Gordon Road for one block and I'm at the store. But sometimes, if I'm in a hurry, I take a shortcut across the schoolyard. A shortcut is quicker because I don't have to take as many steps. Today, you are going to learn about special words that are "shortcuts."

Instruction: Model for the students how to create a shortcut with a word by printing two words like *have not* on a sentence strip in the pocket chart. Then cut out the letters *n* and *o* with scissors. Show students the special "shortcut sign" called an *apostrophe* that takes the place of these letters. Then guide students as they use letter tiles to create additional shortcut words out of longer words. (Additional shortcut words can be found at the end of the minilesson.)

Some words are like shortcuts. We can take two words and make one shorter word out of them that has the same meaning: <u>can't</u> is a shortcut for <u>cannot</u>; <u>he's</u> is a shortcut for <u>he is</u>. We make these shortcut words by printing the two words on a strip of paper and cutting out some of the letters [use scissors to cut out the extra letters]. But then we have to be sure to put in this little shortcut sign [show the tile with the apostrophe] to show that we took out some of the letters.

At some point, you will want to provide students with the correct terminology (i.e., *contractions* and *apostrophes*), but at this point, the "nickname" should help to clarify the concept for students.

After modeling several examples for students, guide them in cutting letters out of words and replacing them with apostrophes. This activity is most effective using the format provided, where students literally cut out the extra letters with scissors and replace them with the apostrophe tile. However, if you find that the cutting exercise detracts from the concept building, try the alternative of providing students with precut letter tiles that they can use to form the words and then take them apart. Start by providing explicit step-by-step instructions, and then gradually allow students to assume more independence. You can use the list of shortcut words (see Table 13) for additional practice.

Writers, please read the words in the boxes at the top of the page of sentence strips. [Invite a student to read the words <u>did</u> <u>not</u>. Ask a student to use the word in a sentence.] Now we're going to make the shortcut word <u>didn't</u>. First, take your scissors and cut out the blank space because we

TABLE 13. A Sampling of "Shortcut" Words

Two Words	"Shortcut" Words
are not	aren't
did not	didn't
does not	doesn't
do not	don't
have not	haven't
is not	isn't
should not	shouldn't
will not	won't
were not	weren't
I am	I'm
I will	I'll
I would	I'd
she will	she'll
he would	he'd
you have	you've
you are	you're
I have	I've
he is	he's
it is	it's
we are	we're
we will	we'll
they have	they've
they would	they'd

are going to combine two words into one. Next, cut out a shortcut sign, which we also call an <u>apostrophe</u>. [Allow time for students to follow the directions.] Now cut out the letter <u>o</u>. Put the shortcut sign in the hole made by the <u>o</u>. Let's spell the shortcut word together: d-i-d-n-shortcut-t. And the whole word is <u>didn't</u>. Does this word fit into the sentence we made with <u>did</u> <u>not</u>? Have the students print the new word on a piece of paper or individual dry-erase board.

Now let's go on to the next set, <u>she is</u>. Don't forget to cut out your shortcut sign and your space between the words because we're putting two words together. Now, this is the tricky part. I'm going to let you and your partner figure out what letter to cut out to make the shortcut word. [Circulate among the students to provide guidance and support.]

As you gradually release control of the activity to the students, have them practice printing the shortcut word each time and creating a context for the word with a sentence. Eventually, they should be able to visualize and print the shortcut word without physically manipulating the letters.

You may want to begin compiling an ongoing reference chart of shortcut words. As with other reference charts, it is most effective if presented interactively—that is, by gradually having students add additional words as they discover them in their own reading and writing.

Application: Provide students with an immediate opportunity—and expectation—for practice with this activity during writing workshop.

Today, during writing workshop, I want you to use at least two different shortcut words in your writing. You may use some of the ones we talked about today, or you may think of others on your own. If you think of others, we can add them to our class chart later. When I come to you, please show me the places where you wrote shortcut words.

Date

Observations

Notes for Future Instruction

Shortcut Words

d	i	d		n	o	t		'

s	h	e		i	s		'

w	e		h	a	v	e		'

h	e		w	i	l	l		'

I		w	o	u	l	d		'

CAPITAL-LETTER WORD SORT

Developmental Levels: Early, Developing, Fluent

Trait: Conventions

Word sorts are a powerful tool for helping students construct knowledge about all kinds of language concepts. This minilesson is designed to clarify for students the difference between words that are capitalized (i.e., proper nouns) and words that are not capitalized (i.e., common nouns). Although the focus of this particular lesson is geared toward emergent and early writers, it also introduces the strategy of word sorting, which may be used to introduce many elements of conventions at all stages of development.

Introduction: Connect this lesson to students' understanding of capital and lowercase letters.

Boys and girls, sometimes we need to use a capital letter at the beginning of a word and sometimes we don't. But how do we know when to use a capital letter? Today, you're going to figure out a way to tell which words need to start with a capital letter and which do not, so you remember this when you write.

Instruction: This activity is a closed word sort because the students are given the sorting instruction, and then they must come up with a generalization to describe the sorting pattern. (In an open sort, the students find their own pattern for sorting.) When possible, I prefer to introduce the words in the context of connected text, although it is not necessary. The words may be presented as a list, as shown on the reproducible at the end of the minilesson. Choose common and proper nouns that the children can relate to—for example, the name of their town or their teacher.

Here is a list of words that we know. [Read them aloud in case there are some words students do not recognize.] Look at the first letter of each word. Sometimes it is a capital letter, and sometimes it is a lowercase letter. Let's list all of the words with capital letters in the first column and all of the words with lowercase letters in the second column. [Invite students to suggest words for each column as you record them. You may want to match up pairs of corresponding common and proper nouns later.]

When the column is complete, it will look something like the following:

Amy	girl
Mr. Smith	teacher
Puff	cat
New York	city
Crest	toothpaste
Ford	car

Ask students if they can add some words of their own to each column.

Now invite students to think of a "writing rule" to help them remember what kinds of words need capital letters. Guide them in developing the rule, but try to use their words as much as possible. The strength of this exercise comes from the students' thinking as they construct their own generalization. (I am somewhat ambivalent about using the word *rule*, given the inconsistencies of the English language. However, it seems to be a label that makes sense to children, especially if you are careful to add the word *usually*.) Students might come up with the following rule or generalization: "When it's a name, it starts with a capital letter."

Application: Developing and fluent writers should be given an opportunity to work in small groups to complete the word sorts independently and come up with their own generalizations. Then the whole class can come together to share their ideas and combine their ideas to add to the "Classroom [or Name of Room] Rules for Writing." Tell students that from this point on, you expect them to always use capital letters when they write the names of people, places, or things.

Word Sort List

Sort the following words into the correct columns:

girl	Amy	teacher	Mr. Smith
Puff	cat	city	New York
toothpaste	Crest	Ford	car

Words That Begin With Capital Letters	Words That Begin With Lowercase Letters
Now think of your own	Now think of your own
Now think of your own	Now think of your own

What's my rule?

SILLY STORIES

Developmental Levels: Early, Developing, Fluent

Traits: Word Choice, Conventions

Silly stories are a highly motivating and engaging way to reinforce vocabulary and parts of speech in writing, based on the party game of "Mad Libs" by Penguin publishers. They involve generating a list of words then inserting the list into an existing story framework. The result is a "silly story."

Introduction: Connect this lesson to students' background experience with choosing effective words in their writing (such as Painting Word Pictures, p. 76). Tell the students that usually they plan the words to fit into the story; however, today they will play a game in which they pick the words first and then put them into the story.

Boys and girls, I can tell that you have been working hard on using "wow" words in your writing and painting "word pictures" in your reader's mind. Like you, good writers carefully plan their stories, and then they think about the best words to use in their stories. But today we're going to do a flip-flop! Today, you don't have to think about your story; you just have to think about the words. You're going to learn about paying attention to different kinds of words.

Instruction: Start by working together to brainstorm the nine missing words from each list.

Today, we're going to play a writing game. I'm going to ask you to help me think of some words, and then we're going to put our words into a story that has already been written. The story might be very funny with our words in it, and it will help us think about the different kinds of words we use.

Silly Story List

(1) A kind of animal (this must be a word that refers to more than one and ends in s): _____

(2) The same kind of animal, but this time, just one: _____

(3) A kind of food: _____

(4) A name of a place (remember that the name of something must begin with a capital letter): _____

*(5) A describing word (a word that tells what something is like): _____
_____*

(6) A name of a girl: _____

(7) Another kind of food: _____

(8) An action word that ends in _ed_: _____

(9) A kind of furniture: _____

NOTES

Date

_____

Observations

_____

_____

_____

_____

_____

_____

_____

_____

_____

Notes for Future Instruction

_____

_____

_____

_____

_____

_____

_____

_____

_____

Animal Report List

(1) A number: _____

(2) A color: _____

(3) A describing word: _____

(4) A kind of food: _____

(5) Another kind of food: _____

(6) A name of a place (needs a capital letter): _____

(7) An action word that ends in _s_: _____

(8) Another action word that ends in _s_: _____

(9) A kind of animal: _____

Invite students to offer words for each prompt. Offer as much explanation and terminology (e.g., part of speech, plural and singular) as you feel appropriate for students. Record their suggestions, and draw students' attention to spelling and capitalization, again, as appropriate. (Remember that the purpose of this activity is to focus on different kinds of words, so don't distract them by discussing every letter. However, it is useful to talk about _ed_ words for verbs, _ly_ words for adverbs, or capital letters for proper nouns.)

Use the templates at the end of the minilesson to complete this activity. Reproduce each template on an overhead transparency so students can read it with you. Insert the numbered words from each list into the appropriate blanks on the templates and create two "silly stories."

Now that you've thought of all these kinds of words, here comes the fun part. We're going to put them into a story that has already been written!

Application: Remind students about the different kinds of words they wrote: different kinds of things, names of things, action words, and describing words. Connect this minilesson to their own writing—thinking about the words we use and using the best words to fit in the text, not just any words or the first words that come to mind.

This highly engaging minilesson will be educational and enjoyable for your students again and again. Always make sure to reinforce the goal of choosing the most interesting and effective words, and linking this activity to word choice in their writing.

Extension: Many commercial resources may be used to access versions of silly stories. Websites such as www.eduplace.com/tales provide an opportunity for students to engage in the activity online. Other books such as _Word Families Ad Libs_ by Learning Resources reinforce phonics concepts as well.

Silly Story Template

Once upon a time there were three (1)_____, a

Mama (2)_____, a Papa (2)_____, and a

Baby (2)_____. Their (3)_____ was too

hot, so they decided to go for a walk in (4)_____

_____ while it cooled.

While they were out, a (5)_____ girl named

(6)_____ came right into their house. She ate all of

the (7)_____ and she (8)_____

_____ all over the house.

Finally, she went to sleep in Baby Bear's (9)_____

_____. When the three (1)_____ came home, they woke

up (6)_____ and sent her home.

Animal Report Template

The googly is an amazing creature. It has (1)_____ legs,

(2)_____ fur, and a (3)_____ tail. It loves to eat

(4)_____ and (5)_____. It lives

in (6)_____. The googly (7) _____ all day

and (8) _____ all night. I think a (9)_____

would be a better pet than a googly.

Date

_____

_____

_____

Observations

_____

_____

_____

_____

_____

_____

_____

_____

_____

_____

Notes for Future Instruction

_____

_____

_____

_____

_____

_____

_____

_____

_____

_____

_____

_____

_____

NAME PART AND DOING PART SENTENCES

Developmental Levels: Early, Developing, Fluent

Trait: Conventions

Telling young children that a sentence is a "complete thought" can be very confusing to them. Many "complete thoughts" are not complete sentences. However, teaching students that a sentence is a special group of words that has a "who" or "what" and an "is" or "does" (in other words, a subject and a predicate) gives them a framework for understanding what a sentence is.

Emergent writers should not be expected to use sentences in their writing when they're not even using words yet. However, in preparation for future writing, oral work with sentences can help provide students with a foundation for understanding sentence structure.

Introduction: Students need to understand the concept of word before they can grasp the definition of a sentence. Introduce the minilesson by telling students that a sentence is a special way to put a group of words together.

Boys and girls, you have been writing words to go along with your pictures. When we write lots of words, we put them together in groups called sentences. A sentence is a special group of words that has two parts. One part of the sentence tells who or what the sentence is about. It's the "name part." The other part of the sentence tells what that person or thing is or does. It's the "doing part."

For example, if I say, "My cat Cookie has a long tail," that group of words is a sentence. "My cat Cookie," is the name part and "has a long tail" is the doing part. Today, you are going to learn how to put words together in sentences.

Instruction: First, give students a few examples of simple sentences and invite them to tell which part of the sentence is the who or what and which part of the sentence is the is or does. Next, give students examples of name parts (e.g., "My Grampa") and invite them to provide doing parts, and give students doing parts (e.g., "played outside") and invite them to add name parts. Then, invite students to create sentences.

Who can give me a sentence about a frog? Who can give me a sentence about going to school?

When students provide complete sentences, praise their efforts. When students provide incomplete sentences, immediately demonstrate how to turn the fragment into a complete sentence. For example, if a student says, "going to school every day," you might say, "That's a great doing part, but it needs a name part." You might complete the sentence by adding something such as "All the boys and girls like going to school every day."

Finally, you may want to show students some pictures from books and ask them to think of sentences about them. Praise complete sentences and help turn fragments into complete sentences.

Application: You may want to assign sentence writing for practice. Provide a topic such as "Halloween" and ask each student to write one sentence about it, or provide a word such as *dog* for each student to include in a written sentence. Have students "pretell" their sentences to writing partners before writing them down. On a subsequent repetition of this minilesson, ask students to write two or three sentences about a topic.

As you circulate among the students to check their sentences, provide immediate support for those students who do not write complete sentences and have them create another one. They should pretell the new sentence before writing it to ensure that it is a complete sentence.

NOTES

Date

Observations

Notes for Future Instruction

TALKING MARKS

Developmental Levels: Developing, Fluent

Trait: Conventions

This minilesson helps students identify dialogue, and it shows how to use quotation marks to separate dialogue from the tag line and other text. Using speech bubbles similar to those found in comic strips is a good way to help students learn to define direct speech.

Introduction: Connect this lesson to Add Some Talking (p. 103).

Boys and girls, you've been working on putting dialogue in your writing to make it sound more interesting and lively for a reader. Remember that dialogue means that people are talking. In writing, we use special talking marks to show when people are talking. Some people call them "macaroni marks" because they look just like two little pieces of macaroni. I've noticed that sometimes you're not sure where to put the talking marks. So today, you're going to learn how to show the talking using talking marks.

Instruction: Look in the newspaper and find an example of a comic strip with speech bubbles to show the students. Talk about how comic strip writers use speech bubbles to show what each character is saying. Read through the comic strip and identify what the characters are saying in each frame.

Make a connection to a previous modeled text, and then turn it into a comic strip for the purpose of identifying the dialogue. Read the text together. Ask the students to identify what, in this example, the little boy says.

> *It's my birthday today. I woke up my mom and dad but they said it's too early. I went down to the kitchen. I saw a birthday cake. I was happy that I got a cake. Then Mom and Dad woke up. I opened my presents.*

If I wanted to make a story into a comic strip, I would start with a picture of a little boy in his pajamas with a speech bubble, like this. And I would put in the speech bubble the part that the little boy says: "Wake up! It's my birthday!" [Sketch the pictures as you think aloud.]

Then I would have a picture of the mom in her bed. Help me decide what I should put in the next speech bubble.

Now, in the last picture, I have a picture of the little boy with his present. I wonder what he would be saying here [see Figure 24].

When we're writing a story, we can't stick speech bubbles in the middle of our writing! So we have to find another way to show the parts where someone is talking. We don't have a picture of the person talking. That's why we have to write, "I shouted" or "my mom said" to show the reader who is talking. And we put the talking marks around the words that we would put in the speech bubble.

Let's look at our writing piece again and add talking marks. Think about which parts we put into the speech bubbles to help us decide where to put the talking marks.

Have the students work with you to mark the dialogue. It is useful to highlight or underline the dialogue to define the beginning and end of each speech. Use an interactive writing approach to help students put in the quotation marks with a colored marker.

It's my birthday today. I went into my mom and dad's room. I whispered, "Wake up. It's my birthday." They didn't wake up. So I yelled, "Wake up! It's my birthday!" My mom groaned, "It's too early. Go back to bed." I went down to the kitchen. I saw a birthday cake. I was happy that I got a cake. Then Mom and Dad woke up. I opened my presents. "Thanks, Mom and Dad," I said.

Application: Ask students to include dialogue in today's writing workshop.

Today, in your writing, I would like you to add some dialogue using talking marks. You may start a new piece or continue to work on a piece in your writing folder. As you write, think about which words you would put in a speech bubble if you were making a comic strip. Be sure to put talking marks at the beginning and end of those words.

Extension: Use a shared writing approach to create a narrative of the comic strip provided.

Date

Observations

Notes for Future Instruction

FIGURE 24. Comic Strip

BE YOUR OWN EDITOR

Developmental Levels: Early, Developing, Fluent

Trait: Conventions

Students should be taught early to take responsibility for their own editing. Encourage students to spell, punctuate, and capitalize "as well as they can" while getting their initial thoughts down on paper. Before students' writing goes public, however, it should be edited for conventions. This lesson teaches a systematic process for beginning editing: the CUPS acronym (*c*apitals, *u*sage, *p*unctuation, *s*pelling), which helps students remember the elements of conventions.

Editing is a process that should take place after all revisions are done. When the writer is satisfied that the writing says what he or she wants it to say, it should be edited for conventions before it is published or shared with an audience. It is not productive to edit the writing of emergent and very early writers because, as previously mentioned, these writers should be focusing on getting their thoughts down on paper. Once students are spelling at least half of the words they write conventionally, I introduce editing. I prefer to use special fine-point markers as editing pens to motivate students to edit and to make corrections visible on the page. These brightly colored "editing pens" are stored in the "CUPS collection."

Introduction: Connect this lesson to the idea of "fixing up" writing to make it easier for others to read. Emphasize that this "fixing up" stage is done after students' writing "sounds" the way they want it to; in other words, after all their revisions are done. Students should still be using bubble gum writing (see Bubble Gum Writing, p. 117), or invented spelling, during drafting; however, when they edit, they should change the bubble gum writing to book writing. The CUPS poster is a visual reminder of the elements of editing (see Figure 25).

Writers, when you draft a piece of writing, you concentrate on getting all your ideas down on paper using bubble gum writing. But book writing is easier for a reader to read because everyone spells words the same way in book writing. Before you publish your writing, you should try to use as much book writing as you can. We fix up the spelling, capital letters, periods, and question marks as well as we can so other readers can read our writing. We call this "editing." Editing is going back into our writing and doing our best to fix up all the CUPS—

FIGURE 25. Editing With CUPS

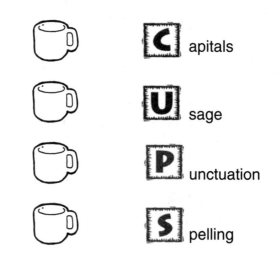

C apitals

U sage

P unctuation

S pelling

capitals, usage, punctuation, and spelling. Today, you are going to learn this step-by-step way to edit your writing.

Instruction: Using an enlarged text from a previous writing lesson, model each step of the editing process (see the step-by-step process at the end of the minilesson).

First, I take out my "framing fingers" [thumb and forefinger in an L shape]. [Frame the first sentence by putting your framing fingers at the beginning and end of the sentence.] Do I have a capital letter inside the left-hand frame and the correct punctuation inside the right-hand frame? If not, I need to use my editing pen to add those in right now.

Now, I read the whole sentence out loud to myself and listen to see if it sounds right. Are there any words that don't sound right? Am I missing any words? Does it sound like my sentence needs to be broken up into smaller sentences?

Next, I'm going to read each word in the sentence out loud and tap it as I read. I'm also making sure I have a spaghetti space between each letter and a meatball space between each word. My pen leaves a little dot under each word as I say it—then I know if I'm missing a word or if I need to add one. As I say and tap each word, I look at it to see if it looks like book writing. If it doesn't look right to me, I just put a circle around it so I can come back and check on it or get help later. [Use a colored editing pen to "tap" each word as you read it aloud. Circle words that don't "look right."]

Finally, repeat the same process with each sentence individually.

Application: Ask each student to choose one finished piece of writing to edit. Distribute editing pens and guide the students through the process as they edit their own work for capital letters, word usage, punctuation, and spelling.

Establish an expectation for students to edit their own writing each time they want to publish a piece.

Date

Observations

Notes for Future Instruction

Be Your Own Editor

1. Frame the first sentence with your fingers.

   • Check for a capital letter at the beginning and punctuation at the end.

2. Read the whole sentence to see if it "sounds right."

   • Does it seem too long? You might need to chop it into shorter sentences.

   • Are there any words that are missing or don't sound right? Trade them or push new ones in.

3. Read it again and tap each word as you read it out loud.

   • Look for spaghetti spaces between the letters and meatball spaces between the words.

   • Circle any words that don't look right to you. You can check them later.

4. Now do the same thing with the rest of the sentences.

CHAPTER 5

Revision: Making Good Writing Even Better

M Y LOCAL READING council's annual Young Authors' Event is a very special occasion at which students whose work has been chosen for publication are invited to read their work in public. It's an exciting evening when kindergarten writers sit on stage alongside high school poets and aspiring novelists, all waiting their turn to be called to the microphone.

One year, I was sitting among the audience of parents, teachers, and other guests, when a first-grade boy with freckles and a cowlick began to read. Suddenly, he paused, obviously confused by something in his story. With a frown on his face, he asked the mistress of ceremonies if she had a pencil he could borrow. She did, and the young man quickly corrected his text. Then he returned to the microphone and resumed reading, much to the delight of his audience.

Later, his teacher came up to me with a broad smile. "You see, Lori, I keep telling my kids that good writers are constantly *revising* their writing! And it works!"

Can beginning writers revise their writing for clarity, style, and effectiveness? Sure, they can. As previously mentioned, experts like Cunningham (Cunningham et al., 2005) and Calkins (2003) contend that the best way for students to learn to be better writers is to go back "into" their writing and make it even better. The minilessons in this chapter offer tools for beginning writers to use as they learn to revisit, review, and revise their writing (see Table 14).

Revision is a part of the writing process that involves adding, deleting, or changing text to make the writing more interesting, clear, or powerful. Revision has nothing to do with fixing spelling or correcting punctuation— that is a process that we typically refer to as "editing." Adults often revise and edit their writing at the same time; however, for young children, it is best to separate these two processes. Routman (2005) cautions us to focus on quality writing before correct conventions. She says that "overattention to grammar and mechanics while composing adversely impacts writing" (p. 160). In other words, writers want their writing to sound the way they want it to sound and convey the message they want it to convey before they worry about spelling and conventions.

TABLE 14. Revision Minilessons at a Glance

Lesson Name	What It Teaches	Developmental Level	Trait	Pages
Adding On at the End	Adding details to the end of a piece of writing	Early Developing Fluent	Ideas	150–151
Pushing In	Inserting words and details in a piece of writing	Early Developing Fluent	Ideas Word choice	152–153
Trading Words	Replacing ordinary words in a piece of writing with more interesting or more powerful words	Developing Fluent	Word choice	154–155
Stretching the Paper	Adding chunks of information within a text	Developing Fluent	Ideas Organization	156
Exploding a Moment	Expanding the most important part in a piece of writing	Fluent	Ideas	157–159
Cutting and Sorting	Reorganizing information in a draft	Developing Fluent	Ideas Organization	160–162
Chopping Out What You Don't Need	Deleting unnecessary information	Developing Fluent	Ideas	163–164
Revising as You Write	Making changes to a text while drafting	Early Developing Fluent	Ideas Organization Voice Word choice Sentence fluency	165–166
The Ice-Cream Cone Rubric	Assessing the quality of a piece of writing	Developing Fluent	Ideas Organization Voice Word choice Sentence fluency	167–170
A Star and a Wish	Peer conferences	Developing Fluent	Ideas Organization Voice Word choice	171–172

Revision is not feasible for emergent writers because they do not yet recognize that writing says the same thing each time it is read (Spandel, 1997). A string of random letters might be read one day as "Grandma is coming to visit" and the next day as "I got a new bike for my birthday." At this stage, we want students to see themselves as writers and to take delight in printing on paper to tell a story. However, even writers at this stage can be encouraged to go back and add more details to their picture, add more "writing," or "tell more" about their picture and writing.

As soon as students can consistently read their writing, they are ready for revision. At the early writing stage, students are making enough letter–sound connections to read their own print. From that point on, they are ready to go back into their writing to revise it. We want early writers to recognize that revisiting a piece of writing to add to it, change it, or otherwise improve it is an integral part of the writing process.

In my work with primary-grade writers, I have found that these students can learn and apply five types of revision:

1. "adding on" more information at the end of the piece;

2. "pushing in" words and short ideas using a caret;

3. "trading" one word or phrase for another;

4. "tucking in" more information in the middle of a piece by "stretching" the paper, or cutting the page apart and pasting in extra paper; and

5. "chopping out" unnecessary words and ideas.

The minilessons in this chapter offer tools for the writer's revision toolbox. The first three minilessons teach basic ways to add to or change text. Even early writers should be able to add information to the end of a piece of writing as demonstrated in the minilesson **Adding On at the End**. In addition, demonstrating how to insert a word or detail with a caret (**Pushing In**) or how to replace one word for another (**Trading Words**) can open up a world of revision for beginning writers. Catchy names, actions, and visual symbols found in these minilessons all help young writers conceptualize, remember, and even want to use these revision tools (Calkins, 2003).

Sometimes writers need to add "chunks" of information to their writing that are too large to insert between the lines. **Stretching the Paper** involves cutting up the text and adding more paper to "tuck in" information. Thus, this tool enables writers to make revisions without recopying the entire piece. Revision teaches students to think critically and creatively about their writing; recopying teaches little more than recopying, at best.

When students know how to "stretch the paper," they can engage in more sophisticated revision techniques such as **Exploding a Moment** (Lane, 1993). Lane describes "exploding a moment" as telling the most interesting or exciting part of the story in "slow motion"; in other words, taking one moment in time and stretching it out over three or four sentences or more.

When the content of students' writing is simply not organized in the most clear and effective way, **Cutting and Sorting** may be used to clarify and reorganize it. This technique simply involves cutting up the text sentence by sentence and pasting it back down in a more coherent order.

Even the most fluent writers are reluctant to remove even one precious word of their text. After all, considering the amount of effort that it takes for a primary-grade writer to get each word on paper, it is obvious why **Chopping Out What You Don't Need** is the most challenging revision strategy. For this reason, I teach students about adding information early on, but I don't teach them about deleting information until at least the developing and fluent stages.

Revising as You Write shows students how to make changes as they draft a piece of writing. In this minilesson, students learn that they don't need to wait until they have finished writing the whole piece to make changes. Avery (1993) introduces revising to her first graders on the first day of school, and assures them that "All writers change their minds" (p. 181). Students need to realize that it is acceptable to change a word, take out a detail, or add in an extra thought while they are writing; they can simply cross out what they don't want and keep going. Once students have a repertoire of these revision tools, they may apply any of the techniques as they write.

It's important for us to explicitly model and demonstrate these processes so students can see how to go back into a piece of writing they may have already "finished." We should take advantage of frequent opportunities to go back and add to or rework existing modeled writing samples, thinking aloud as we add, change, or delete sections of text to make the writing more interesting, clear, or powerful. Then, the students need opportunities to practice these techniques. We often find that it's easier for writers—of any age—to revise someone else's work than to revise our own. Giving the students an opportunity to work with a partner to revise a piece of sample writing, for example, enables them to practice a technique before applying it to their own writing.

Rewriting fatigue is only one of the reasons why revision is so painful for students. Another reason is that revision is different from other learning processes students undertake in school. When students have to redo math or social studies questions, it's usually because the answers are wrong or incomplete. But revision is something writers do to *good* writing to make it *even better.*

Writers do lots of writing that never gets beyond the first draft stage. Just like artists choose their best works of art and dancers choose their best routines to share with an audience, writers choose their best pieces of writing to share with an audience. And just like the dancer keeps on practicing that routine to make it as good as it can possibly be, the writer keeps on revising that piece of writing to make it as good as it can possibly be.

I tell students that revision is like a compliment to a piece of writing; it makes our best work *even better*. Requiring students to be selective about which pieces of writing to revise and publish helps reinforce the idea of choosing the best and making it better.

Another problem with revision is that most of our students truly believe that their first draft of writing is perfect just the way it is. Otherwise, they wouldn't have written it that way. Our role is to guide students in discovering ways to make their "perfect" writing *even better*. Through individual writing conferences, we can support students in honing their revision tools. For example, the TAG conference (see chapter 1, p. 27) provides an efficient and effective structure for conferring with young writers. Explicit instruction, high expectations, and supportive scaffolding are needed to extend students' reach as writers. Our roles as teacher, mentor, and coach work not only to help students improve one particular piece of writing but also to add strategies to their writing toolboxes to help improve *all* their writing.

The Ice-Cream Cone Rubric is a tool for helping students analyze the strengths and weaknesses of a piece of writing—the writing of others and, ultimately, their own. The minilesson also gives students a language for talking about writing, which will help them when they conduct "a star and a wish" conferences with one another. In the minilesson **A Star and a Wish**, students tell a partner one thing they like, the equivalent of a "star," about the piece of writing and then describe one thing they "wish" the writer had done.

Just how much revision can we expect of beginning writers? In almost any piece of student writing, we can usually identify half a dozen teaching points, or a whole array of areas for improvement. But for beginning writers, *one* change is probably adequate. When teaching revision, we need to remember that our job is not to mold a great literary marvel; it is to support a developing writer.

ADDING ON AT THE END

Developmental Levels: Early, Developing, Fluent

Trait: Ideas

The simplest form of revision is adding details to the end of a piece of writing. As soon as writers are able to read their own writing, encourage them to begin revision by adding on to their writing. Guide students in revising by asking questions that generate additional details for the writing.

Introduction: Connect this lesson to Sticky Dot Details (p. 57).

Last week, Jessica asked me if she could have another dot so she could add another sticky dot detail to her writing. I was so pleased to give her another dot because adding details to a piece of writing is something good writers do all the time. It's something we do to make a good piece of writing even better! Today, you're all going to learn how you can make a good piece of writing even better by adding a detail at the end.

Instruction: Demonstrate how to add a detail to the end of a piece of writing using modeled writing from a previous lesson.

Here is a piece of writing that I did a while ago:

My Summer Holidays
I went camping in the mountains. I saw a bear.

I think I can make this piece of writing better by adding more details at the end. Maybe I could add a detail about what the bear looked like. Or I might add a detail about how I felt when I saw the bear. I think I'm going to add that I was really, really scared.

My Summer Holidays
I went camping in the mountains. I saw a bear. I was really, really scared.

You know, I probably could even add some more details to the end of my story. But I can't think of any to add. Maybe one of you can help me out. Can anyone think of a question to ask me about my story? [Allow students to ask questions and choose one to respond to.] Those are some great questions. I think I'm going to add on an answer to Jamie's question about where the bear was.

My Summer Holidays

I went camping in the mountains. I saw a bear. I was really, really scared. The bear was on the side of the road.

Application: Have students choose a piece of writing that they have already finished from their writing folders. Then, have students pair up with a "buddy" for "knee-to-knee" conferences. The buddy might ask questions of the writer, or simply offer suggestions for additional details. (A routine used in the minilesson A Star and a Wish, described later in this chapter, is good for buddy conferences.) Often a writer assumes the reader has the same background knowledge as he or she does. Buddy conferences point out where the gaps might be in a piece of writing and help a writer learn to see his or her writing from the point of view of a reader.

NOTES

Date

_____

Observations

_____
_____
_____
_____
_____
_____
_____
_____
_____

Notes for Future Instruction

_____
_____
_____
_____
_____
_____
_____
_____
_____
_____
_____

Date

Observations

Notes for Future Instruction

PUSHING IN

Developmental Levels: Early, Developing, Fluent

Traits: Ideas, Word Choice

In this minilesson, students learn to "push in," or insert, words, groups of words, or even whole sentences into a draft.

Introduction: Connect this lesson to Adding On at the End (p. 150).

We have been practicing adding on details at the end of a piece of writing. But sometimes we want to add a word or a detail in the middle of a piece of writing. Sometimes we can think of "wow" words or important ideas that we want to add so our writing makes more sense or is more descriptive. Today, you are going to learn how to "push in" new words and details anywhere in your writing. [Put your fingertips together to form a point and gesture to simulate "pushing in" to provide additional reinforcement for the concept.]

Instruction: Using a piece of existing writing, demonstrate how to insert a word or detail with a caret.

When we want to add words and ideas into the middle of our writing, we use a sign that looks like this little upside-down v to push them in. [Draw a caret.] This sign is called a <u>caret</u>, and you can see that it's almost like the shape of the carrot we eat! We put the caret in the spot where we want to add the word and then write the word above it, just like this. [Indicate where you will add information to the writing sample.] I think I'd like to add the word <u>long</u> before <u>skinny</u> to help paint a picture of how Cookie's tail looks. And I'd better push in "one day" to show that Cookie doesn't hop in the bathtub every day. That will help make my writing more clear for the reader. [See Figure 26.]

Application: Have students go into their writing folders and select a piece of finished writing. Instruct them to look for a place where they can "push in" a more interesting or more powerful word, or add an important detail to help tell the story. As you circulate around the classroom, have students point out their revisions to you.

FIGURE 26. Pushing In Sample

My cat Cookie has bald
eyebrows and a ^long skmny tail.
She likes water and ^one day she jumped
in the bath tub. Cookie is
a funny cat.

TRADING WORDS

Developmental Levels: Developing, Fluent

Trait: Word Choice

This minilesson may be used to teach students how to revise their writing by replacing words or phrases with more interesting or more powerful words.

Introduction: Connect this lesson to Adding On at the End and Pushing In (see pp. 150 and 152, respectively).

You are doing such a good job with adding details to the end of your writing or "pushing in" words in the middle of your writing. But what if you want to change something in your writing? Just because you used certain words in your writing, it doesn't mean you're stuck with those words forever. Maybe you learned a new word or thought of some better words you want to use instead. Today, you're going to learn how to trade words or ideas in your writing for other words or ideas. [The gesture for "trading" is a horizontal slash with your hand to represent the line you draw through the old text to replace it with the new.]

Instruction: Help the students understand the concept of "trading" and discuss with them why you might want to "trade" words in the text. Then use a piece of existing modeled writing to demonstrate how to do it.

The other day in the lunchroom, I heard Spiro say, "I'll trade you my baloney sandwich for your ham sandwich." And the girls are always trading stickers from their sticker books. Sometimes we take something we already have and trade it for something else we may want. That's what trading is. And we can trade words and ideas in our writing, just like we trade stickers or sandwiches!

Sometimes after I've finished a piece of writing, I think of another word I want to use, or I hear a word from another piece of writing, and I think, "I wish I had used that word." Well, I can! I can just trade the word in my writing with another word I like better. All I have to do is cross out the old word and write the new word above it.

Look at what I wrote about my cat Cookie. I'd like to trade that ordinary word <u>jumped</u> for <u>hopped</u>. And I just read a wow word, <u>hilarious</u>; I'm going to trade it with this ordinary word, <u>funny</u>. [See Figure 27.]

Application: Have students go into their writing folders and choose a finished piece of writing. Instruct them to look for at least one place where they can practice "trading" one word for another one that is more interesting or powerful. As you circulate around the classroom, have them point out their "trades" to you.

Extension: When students are comfortable with trading individual words, introduce trading phrases, sentences, or larger "chunks" of information.

FIGURE 27. Trading Words Sample

My cat Cookie has bald eyebrows and a skinny tail. She likes coffee. One day she ~~jumped~~ hopped in the bath tub. I think Cookie is a ~~funny~~ hilarious cat.

Date

Observations

Notes for Future Instruction

STRETCHING THE PAPER

Developmental Levels: Developing, Fluent

Traits: Ideas, Organization

Often writers revise their writing by inserting large "chunks" of information. This lesson helps you model for students the revision process by cutting a piece of writing and pasting in extra paper so the writer can "stretch the paper" and "tuck in" ideas in the middle of the text.

Introduction: Connect this lesson to Pushing In (see p. 152).

I've noticed that you have been doing some very interesting work with "pushing in" words and short details into your writing. But the other day, Lucas wanted to put a whole bunch of information into the middle of his story, and he didn't have room to write it all. Today, you're going to learn how to "tuck in" a chunk of information into the middle of a piece of writing by "stretching" the paper.

Instruction: Use an existing text that was written for another modeled writing lesson (such as the example below) or create a new text for this lesson, to model this revision process for students.

> My cat Cookie has bald eyebrows and a long, skinny tail. She likes to drink coffee. One day she jumped in the bathtub. Cookie is a funny cat, but I love her a lot.

When I had "a star and a wish" conference with my writing buddy, she asked me how Cookie drinks coffee. You know what Cookie does? She dips her paw into a cup of cold coffee and then she licks her paw! I think I would like to add that detail to my story. But it doesn't belong at the end, and I don't have room to "push in" that much information in the middle. So I need to "stretch" my paper.

Demonstrate for the students how to use scissors to cut apart the text between "She likes to drink coffee" and "One day she jumped in the bathtub." Next, tape an extra piece of paper in the space. Then, write the following on the blank paper: "You know what she does? She dips her paw into a cup that's already cooled and then licks her paw!" Finally, tape the remainder of the story back on to the end.

Application: Students may need lots of support for this technique before they can use it independently. Provide opportunities for students to practice on sample texts.

EXPLODING A MOMENT

Developmental Level: Fluent

Trait: Ideas

"Exploding a moment" is a writing strategy developed by Barry Lane (1993) to help students focus and elaborate on a key event or detail in a piece of writing. This is a useful strategy to teach when students begin writing the "breakfast to bed" stories, which are typically a string of events from the beginning of the day to the end of the day without much elaboration and detail.

Introduction: Connect this lesson to the concept of adding chunks of information to "stretch" a piece of writing (see Stretching the Paper, p. 156).

Writers, you have been practicing "tucking" details into the middle of your stories. Today, you're going to learn how to tuck in special details to make your stories more exciting. When we tell a story in writing, we want readers to pay attention to the most exciting or interesting part. That's why we need to elaborate or add details to the parts we want readers to pay attention to. One of the ways to elaborate is to slow down an interesting part and tell every detail, just like slow motion in a movie or television show. We call this technique "exploding a moment" because we use three or four sentences to tell about one specific moment in time.

Instruction: Create or find an example of a text that consists mainly of a list of events. Following is an example:

It was Thanksgiving. I got up in the morning and put on my Pats sweatshirt. Then the whole family piled into the van to go to Grandma's. On the way, Dad crashed the van into a tree. Luckily, we could still drive it. We got to Grandma's and had a turkey dinner. Then we came home.

What's the most exciting part of my story? Crashing the van into a tree! But I didn't tell you any details about it. In fact, I told you just as much about what I was wearing! I need to "explode the moment" about crashing the van into the tree, so you, as my readers, know that it's the important part of my story.

I prefer to conduct this lesson as a shared writing activity in which the students compose the text with me. However, it may also be conducted as a modeled writing lesson and "think aloud" as you compose.

Date

Observations

Notes for Future Instruction

N O T E S

Date

Observations

Notes for Future Instruction

Let's think about the one minute in time when the van crashed into a tree. What do you suppose happened? [As the students generate ideas, add them to the story. Guide students in recounting step-by-step details. See Figure 28.]

Now it's clear what the most exciting part of the story is because we gave it lots of detail. We elaborated on it by telling every little step that happened. When we slow down and add details, we let the reader know that this is the exciting part of the story.

Application: This is an appropriate time for a prompted writing assignment to ensure that the students have an opportunity to apply the writing technique. Provide guided practice by giving the students a piece of text such as the example at the end of the minilesson and asking them to work in pairs to "explode" the most exciting moment.

FIGURE 28. Exploding a Moment Sample

It was Thanksgiving. I got up in the morning and put on my Pats sweatshirt. Then the whole family piled into the van. On the way, a deer ran onto the road. Dad slammed on the brakes. We all screamed! The van swerved and slid right into a tree by the road side.

Luckily we could still drive it. We got to Grandma's and had a turkey dinner. Then we went back home.

158

Exploding a Moment Sample

In the winter, I like to go sledding with my brother. We take turns going down the hill to see who can go fastest. One day I went backwards down the hill. I fell off the sled and into a big pile of snow. I was covered with snow, but I was still the fastest.

CUTTING AND SORTING

Developmental Levels: Developing, Fluent

Traits: Ideas, Organization

Sometimes students write extended pieces of writing but have several sentences in random order. This minilesson is designed to help writers reorganize their writing by cutting apart the sentences and placing and gluing them in a more logical sequence.

Introduction: Connect this minilesson to the concept of cutting up a piece of writing to "stretch" the paper (see Stretching the Paper, p. 156).

Last week when Stephanie and I were reading over her writing, we thought some of her details were in the wrong place. But how could she change them after the piece was already written? You've already been practicing cutting up a piece of writing to stretch the paper. Today, you're going to learn how to cut up a piece of writing and put it back together, almost like a puzzle.

Instruction: Find a piece of writing in which the details are in some disorder (such as the following example) or create your own in order to model for the students how to cut up a piece of writing and put it back together. Print the text in large print on chart paper.

> My Grandma's Cat
>
> My grandma has a cat. It had a baby. My grandma's cat scratched me. The baby is black and scared a lot. The cats knocked down the Christmas tree. The big cat is kind of mean. There was glass all over the place.

This piece of writing was done by a second-grade student. It's got all kinds of ideas about "My Grandma's Cat," but we aren't always sure which details are about the grandma's cat and which are about the kitten. Let's cut apart this piece of writing and think about putting the sentences back together in an order that makes more sense to us. [Cut the sentences into strips as below.]

My grandma has a cat.

It had a baby.

My grandma's cat scratched me.

The baby is black and scared a lot.

The cats knocked down the Christmas tree.

The big cat is kind of mean.

There was glass all over the place.

I'm going to put all the details about my grandma's cat together, and I'm going to put all the details about the baby cat together. Then I can leave all the details about the Christmas tree together. [Paste the individual sentences in the new order, as follows:]

My grandma has a cat.

My grandma's cat scratched me.

The big cat is kind of mean.

It had a baby.

The baby is black and scared a lot.

The cats knocked down the Christmas tree.

There was glass all over the place.

Now my writing makes more sense because all the details that belong together are put together.

Application: Find or create a new example of writing in which the details are out of order such as the one at the end of the minilesson. Provide each pair of students with a copy of the example to cut apart and reassemble.

Extension: When students are comfortable with the cut-and-sort process, you may want to model "sorting and stretching," which involves leaving spaces between the lines to write more details.

Cutting and Sorting Sample

I love to visit my grandma and gramps. My grandma bakes buns and cookies. My gramps has a shop with lots of tools. Grandma plays cards with me. Gramps has a tickly beard. Grandma always lets me win. My gramps says he can fix anything but a broken heart.

CHOPPING OUT WHAT YOU DON'T NEED

Developmental Levels: Developing, Fluent

Trait: Ideas

When students read over their completed drafts, they sometimes realize that they included details that don't fit or don't add to the main idea. This minilesson demonstrates for students how to "chop out" unnecessary information. Deleting information is the most difficult form of revision for the beginning writer (and perhaps *any* writer) because they put so much thought and effort into every word. However, for more sophisticated writers, learning to remove information is every bit as important as learning to add it.

Introduction: Connect this lesson to students' previous learning about revision.

You have all been working on revising your writing by adding information to the end or in the middle of your paper. But sometimes, instead of adding information, we find we have information we don't need in our writing. Maybe it doesn't fit with our main idea or it repeats something we've already said. Today, you are going to learn how to "chop" information you don't need.

Instruction: Show students an example of writing with unnecessary details such as the following example, and invite them to point out information they think the writer doesn't need.

My Broken Ankle

One winter day, my family and I were going for a walk. Suddenly I tripped and fell on the ground. My ankle hurt so much! My dad had to rush me to the hospital. I got a pretty pink cast. I could not walk very well, but it was okay. When I got home I just lay on the couch and watched TV. My favorite show is "American Idol." When it was suppertime, my mom made pizza. I ate every single crumb left on my plate. After about a month, the doctor took off my cast. I was glad to move my ankle again.

Think about what this piece of writing is all about—when the writer broke her ankle. Are there any details that aren't about what happened when she broke her ankle? For example, is it important to the story to include what her favorite show is? This writer could "chop" that detail by simply crossing it out. [Take students' suggestions and cross out the unnecessary detail as noted below.]

My Broken Ankle

One winter day, my family and I were going for a walk. Suddenly I tripped and fell on the ground. My ankle hurt so much! My dad had to rush me to the hospital. I got a pretty pink cast. I could not walk very well, but it was okay. When I got home I just lay on the couch and watched TV. ~~My favorite show is "American Idol."~~ When it was suppertime, my mom made pizza. I ate every single crumb left on my plate. After about a month, the doctor took off my cast. I was glad to move my ankle again.

Application: You may want to provide students with a piece of writing other than their own to practice "chopping" information before they perform this "surgery" on their own. After students have had ample opportunities to practice this routine on sample texts, tell them to start looking for places in their writing where they can cut information that doesn't need to be there.

REVISING AS YOU WRITE

Developmental Levels: Early, Developing, Fluent

Traits: Ideas, Organization, Voice, Word Choice, Sentence Fluency

Writers often make changes to their writing while they are in the process of writing. Students need to learn that they don't have to wait till they have finished a draft to make revisions. This lesson models the use of revision tools addressed in this chapter—pushing in, trading, chopping out—while they are writing.

Introduction: Explain to students that writers constantly revise as they write.

Do you know that writers often change their minds while they are writing? What if you think of a better word to use or a better way to say something? What if you want to add a detail or take out something you've said? You can just change them as you go, by "pushing in" or trading.

Instruction: Think aloud as you model composing a piece of writing. As you write, make one or two revisions. Model rereading as you write.

"When I was riding on Splash Mountain, there were some little tiny ducks swimming along in the water." I'm going to cross out "little tiny ducks" and write "ducklings." "I picked the ducklings"—no, I'm going to say "scooped"—"I scooped them up one by one and put them on the edge so they wouldn't get hurt." I think I want to say that idea about them getting hurt earlier in the piece. I'm going to push in the sentence, "I was afraid they would get hurt." [See Figure 29.]

Application: Encourage students to make changes as they write, and praise students who make changes to content and craft while they are drafting. In future minilessons, take advantage of frequent opportunities to model "revising as you write."

Date

Observations

Notes for Future Instruction

FIGURE 29. Revising as You Write Sample

When I was riding on Splash Mountain, there were some ~~little tiny~~ ~~ducks~~ ducklings swimming along in the water.^ I ~~picked~~ scooped them up one by one and put them safely^ on the edge. ~~so they wouldn't get hurt.~~

^I was afraid they would get hurt, so

THE ICE-CREAM CONE RUBRIC

Developmental Levels: Developing, Fluent

Traits: Ideas, Organization, Voice, Word Choice, Sentence Fluency

Rubrics are important tools for assessing students' writing because they show what writing traits look like at various levels (Spandel, 2003). They also provide a language for talking about writing. The writing rubric used in this minilesson uses an analogy to an ice-cream cone: The rubric equates adequate or satisfactory writing to a single-scoop cone, exemplary writing to a triple-scoop cone with sprinkles, and inadequate writing to an empty cone. Most students can relate to this analogy for satisfactory, exemplary, and inadequate performance. This minilesson demonstrates how students can use the rubric to assess other people's writing, and as they become more sophisticated, to assess and improve their own.

Introduction: Connect this minilesson to A Star and a Wish (p. 171). During writing conferences, students can use this rubric as a guide for deciding whether a piece of writing is "wow" (exemplary), "pretty good" (satisfactory), or "needs some help" (inadequate).

When we do star and wish conferences, we get ideas from someone else about our writing. Our writing buddies tell us some good things, or "stars," about our writing and some things they wish we would tell more about. Today, you are going to learn how to give your own writing stars and wishes, using a special chart or rubric that will help you think about whether your writing is "wow," "pretty good," or "needs some help."

Instruction: The three-level rubric shown at the end of the minilesson is based on five of the six traits of effective writing: (1) ideas, (2) organization, (3) word choice, (4) voice, and (5) sentence fluency (conventions are not included because they deal with editing as opposed to revision). Teach the rubric one trait at a time and gather writing samples to model each trait. Read aloud the piece of writing together. Then have students consider where it fits on the rubric and hold up one, two, or three fingers to represent (1) writing that needs help, (2) pretty good writing, or (3) wow writing. If the writing receives a "3," then the writer probably doesn't need to focus his or her revision on that trait. If the writing receives a "1," use the shared writing process to revise that trait. If the piece gets a "2," it's up to the writer to decide

Date

Observations

Notes for Future Instruction

whether he or she wants to revise the writing to make it a piece of wow writing. It's OK if students assign different numbers to a piece, as long as they can explain why they chose that number.

This chart is what I call The Ice-Cream Cone Rubric. If you go to the ice-cream store and ask for an ice-cream cone and you get a cone with one scoop, that's OK. It's just what you asked for. But if you get three scoops with sprinkles, then that's a "wow"! And if you ask for an ice-cream cone but just get a cone with no ice cream in it, then you need some help, right?

Wow!	Pretty Good	Needs Some Help
(3)	(2)	(1)

This rubric will help us determine if a piece of writing is "wow," "pretty good," or "needs some help."

Introduce one trait on the rubric at a time and read aloud the criteria:

Wow!	Pretty Good	Needs Some Help
(3)	(2)	(1)
My writing has a main idea and lots of good details about the topic.	My writing has a main idea and some details about the topic.	My writing doesn't have a lot of details on the topic.

Use some pieces of writing that exemplify different levels on the rubric for each of the traits. Think aloud as you plot each piece of writing on the rubric.

Here is a piece of writing all about pigs.

Pig Report

Pigs live on farms. They eat grain and water. Bacon, ham, sausage and pork chops come from pigs. Pigs are the smartest farm animal. They can sometimes learn tricks, like opening a gate. Pigs are not really dirty. They just go in the mud to keep cool.

I think I would give this writing three fingers, wow. It has a main idea—pigs—and all the details are about pigs. But what makes it a wow piece of writing for me is that there are surprising details about pigs. I didn't know pigs could learn tricks.

Application: Provide additional samples for the students, from this book or from your own collections and invite the students to "score" them. Then ask the students to choose a piece of writing from their own collections and score it as a 1, 2, or 3.

Extension: When students become familiar with the scoring process, invite them to find a piece of their own writing that would be a 1 or 2, and ask them to try to revise the writing to make it a 3.

N O T E S

Date

Observations

Notes for Future Instruction

The Ice-Cream Cone Rubric

Wow! (3)	Pretty Good (2)	Needs Some Help (1)
This writing has a main idea with lots of interesting details.	This writing has a main idea and some details.	This writing doesn't have a lot of details. It's hard to tell what the main idea is.
The lead hooks the reader's attention and the end wraps up the piece neatly.	There is an OK beginning, middle, and end.	There isn't really a beginning or end, just a middle.
This writing has lots of personality.	This writing sounds nice and pleasant.	This writing sounds a bit like a robot.
There are lots of wow words.	There are a few wow words.	All the words are pretty ordinary.
There are some long and some short sentences.	The sentences are all about the same length.	The whole piece is just one sentence.

Marvelous Minilessons for Teaching Beginning Writing, K–3 by Lori Jamison Rog. © 2007 International Reading Association.
May be copied for classroom use.

A STAR AND A WISH

Developmental Levels: Developing, Fluent

Traits: Ideas, Organization, Voice, Word Choice

Even the youngest students can respond to one another's writing by offering a compliment (a "star") and a question (a "wish") about the content. Although this exercise is oral, it can be a starting point for the revision process for developing and fluent writers. Teach and practice this routine during author's chair (see chapter 1 for a description of author's chair). Later, the students can engage in their own "star and wish" conferences. Remind the students that these are "knee-to-knee" conferences where students face each other to listen to the writer read. ("Hip-to-hip" conferences, where the students sit beside each other, tend to focus more on conventions because the partner can see the text along with the writer.) The writer reads his or her piece to a partner, and the partner responds with a compliment and a question or suggestion. Because writers read their work, each partner must listen carefully and focus on the content of the writing, not the mechanics.

Introduction: Invite students to make a personal connection to their own experiences by reminding students that writers like to receive positive feedback about their writing.

We all like to read our writing out loud in author's chair, especially when other people tell us all the things they like about our writing. It makes us feel good about our writing. When we listen to someone else's writing, we can tell the writer something we like about his or her writing and make the writer feel good too. Saying what we liked about someone else's writing is kind of like giving the writer a "star" for his or her writing! Sometimes we can give the writer a "wish" for his or her writing, too—maybe something we wish we knew more about or a question we would like to ask the writer about the writing. Today, you are going to learn how to give another writer "a star and a wish."

Instruction: Read aloud a sample of student writing, and think aloud as you follow it with a "star" and a "wish."

Here is a piece that one student wrote about turtles.

Turtles eat. Turtles swim. Turtles sleep. Turtles are green. Turtles stick out their head. Turtles have bodies. Turtles have heads. Turtles have everything. Some turtles live outdoors.

My star for this writer is that he has lots of details on his topic of turtles. Everything in this writing is about turtles. He didn't wander off and talk about going to the beach or something like that. But I wish he would have told me what turtles eat. And I wish he would tell what he means by "everything."

Now invite the students to give you a star and a wish about a piece of your writing.

Remember this piece of writing about my cat Cookie?

My cat Cookie has bald eyebrows and a skinny tail. She likes to drink coffee. One day, she jumped in the bathtub. I think Cookie is a funny cat.

What can you tell me that you like about this piece? Those are my stars. Now can you give me a wish—something you wish I had told in this piece?

Application: It may be necessary to guide the students in order to help them build language to talk about the writing. For example, "You read it in a good voice" is not a useful star. You want the students to focus on the writing, not the writer. In addition, "I didn't like..." is not an appropriate wish. Prompts like "I like the part where..." or "I wish you had told..." or "I'd like to know more about..." can help students get started.

Why did you like that part about Cookie drinking coffee? Because it's a surprising detail? Do you like the way I wrapped up the piece with how I feel about Cookie—just like the bow on a present?

Take plenty of opportunities to practice star and wish conferences together as a group before expecting students to engage in them on their own.

Extension: When students have acquired a repertoire of revision strategies, encourage them to make a revision to their writing based on their star and wish conference.

Atwell, N. (1998). *In the middle: New understandings about writing, reading, and learning* (2nd ed.). Portsmouth, NH: Heinemann.

Avery, C. (1993). *...And with a light touch: Learning about reading, writing, and teaching first graders*. Portsmouth, NH: Heinemann.

Bear, D.R., Invernizzi, M., Templeton, S., & Johnston, F. (2000). *Words their way: Word study for phonics, vocabulary, and spelling* (2nd ed.). Upper Saddle River, NJ: Merrill.

Brown, C.W. (1996). Listening to the experts in my first-grade classroom. *Teaching & Change, 3*(2), 115–129.

Bryson, B. (2003). *A short history of nearly everything*. Toronto, ON: Doubleday Canada.

Burns, M.S., Griffin, P., & Snow, C.E. (Eds.). (1999). *Starting out right: A guide to promoting children's reading success*. Washington, DC: National Academy Press.

Calkins, L.M. (1986). *The art of teaching writing*. Portsmouth, NH: Heinemann.

Calkins, L.M. (2003). *Units of study for primary writing: A yearlong curriculum*. Portsmouth, NH: Heinemann.

Clarke, L.K. (1988). Invented versus traditional spelling in first graders' writings: Effects on learning to spell and read. *Research in the Teaching of English, 22*(3), 281–309.

Clay, M.M. (1976). *What did I write? Beginning writing behaviour*. Portsmouth, NH: Heinemann.

Clay, M.M. (1991). *Becoming literate: The construction of inner control*. Portsmouth, NH: Heinemann.

Culham, R. (2003). *6+1 Traits of writing: The complete guide (grades 3 and up)*. New York: Scholastic.

Culham, R. (2005). *6+1 Traits of writing: The complete guide for the primary grades*. New York: Scholastic.

Cunningham, P.M. (1995). *Phonics they use: Words for reading and writing* (2nd ed.). New York: HarperCollins.

Cunningham, P.M., & Allington, R.L. (1998). *Classrooms that work: They can all read and write* (2nd ed.). Boston: Allyn & Bacon.

Cunningham, P.M., Cunningham, J.W., Hall, D.P., & Moore, S. (2005). *Writing the four-blocks way*. Greensboro, NC: Carson-Dellosa.

Dahl, K.L., & Farnan, N. (1998). *Children's writing: Perspectives from research*. Newark, DE: International Reading Association; Chicago: National Reading Conference.

Dahl, K.L., & Freppon, P.A. (1995). A comparison of inner-city children's interpretations of reading and writing instruction in the early grades in skills-based and whole language classrooms. *Reading Research Quarterly, 30*(1), 50–74.

Diederich, P. (1974). *Measuring growth in English*. Urbana, IL: National Council of Teachers of English.

Education Department of Western Australia. (1994). *Writing developmental continuum (First Steps)*. Portsmouth, NH: Heinemann.

Elbow, P. (2004). Writing first! *Educational Leadership, 62*(2), 8–13.

Fisher, B. (1995). Writing workshop in a first grade classroom. *Teaching Pre K–8, 26*(3), 66–68.

Fitzpatrick, J. (1999). *Teaching beginning writing: Lesson plans to support five developmental writing stages*. Huntington Beach, CA: Creative Teaching Press.

Fletcher, R., & Portalupi, J. (2001). *Writing workshop: The essential guide*. Portsmouth, NH: Heinemann.

Fox, M. (1993). *Radical reflections: Passionate opinions on teaching, learning & living.* San Diego, CA: Harcourt Brace.

Freeman, M.S. (1998). *Teaching the youngest writers: A practical guide.* Gainesville, FL: Maupin House.

Fry, E.B., Kress, J.E., & Fountoukidis, D.L. (2000). *The reading teacher's book of lists* (4th ed.). Paramus, NJ: Prentice Hall.

Gentry, J.R. (1985). You can analyze developmental spelling—and here's how to do it! *Early Years K–8, 15*(9), 44–45.

Gillet, J.W., & Kita, M.J. (1979). Words, kids, and categories. *The Reading Teacher, 32*(5), 538–546.

Gould, J.S., & Gould, E. (1999). *Four Square Writing Method: A unique approach to teaching basic writing skills for grades 1–3.* Carthage, IL: Teaching and Learning.

Graves, D.H. (1983). *Writing: Teachers and children at work.* Exeter, NH: Heinemann.

Graves, D.H. (1994). *A fresh look at writing.* Portsmouth, NH: Heinemann.

Graves, D.H., & Hansen, J. (1983). The author's chair. *Language Arts, 60*(2), 176–183.

Hall, D.P., & Cunningham, P.M. (1997). *Month-by-month reading, writing, and phonics for kindergarten: Systematic, multilevel instruction for kindergarten.* Greensboro, NC: Carson-Dellosa.

Hall, D.P., & Williams, E. (2003). *Writing mini-lessons for kindergarten: The building-blocks model.* Greensboro, NC: Carson-Dellosa.

Hansen, J. (1987). *When writers read.* Portsmouth, NH: Heinemann.

Hillocks, G., Jr. (1986). *Research on written composition: New directions for teaching.* Urbana, IL: National Council of Teachers of English.

International Reading Association & National Association for the Education of Young Children. (1998). *Learning to read and write: Developmentally appropriate practices for children* (Position statement). Newark, DE; Washington, DC: Authors.

Lane, B. (1993). *After the end: Teaching and learning creative revision.* Portsmouth, NH: Heinemann.

Martinez, M., & Teale, W.H. (1988). Reading in a kindergarten classroom library. *The Reading Teacher, 41*(6), 568–573.

Marzano, R.J., Norford, J.S., Paynter, D.E., Pickering, D.J., & Gaddy, B.B. (2001). *A handbook for classroom instruction that works.* Alexandria, VA: Association for Supervision and Curriculum Development.

McClanahan, R. (2000). *Word painting: A guide to writing more descriptively.* Cincinnati, OH: Writers' Digest Books.

Morris, D. (1993). The relationship between children's concept of word in text and phoneme awareness in learning to read: A longitudinal study. *Research in the Teaching of English, 27*(2), 133–154.

National Institute of Child Health and Human Development. (2000). *Report of the National Reading Panel. Teaching children to read: An evidence-based assessment of the scientific research literature on reading and its implications for reading instruction* (NIH Publication No. 00-4769). Washington, DC: U.S. Government Printing Office.

Owl Online Writing Lab, Purdue University. (n.d.). Transitional devices. Retrieved July 17, 2006, from http://owl.english.purdue.edu/handouts/print/general/gl_transition.html

Piaget, J. (1952). *The origins of intelligence in children.* New York: International Universities Press.

Qualifications and Curriculum Authority. (1998). *Can do better: Raising boys' achievement in English.* London: Author.

Ray, K.W., & Cleaveland, L.B. (2004). *About the authors: Writing workshop with our youngest writers.* Portsmouth, NH: Heinemann.

Richgels, D.J. (1995). Invented spelling ability and printed word learning in kindergarten. *Reading Research Quarterly, 30*(1), 96–109.

Roberts, J. (2004). *25 prewriting graphic organizers and planning sheets: Must-have tools to help all students gather and organize their thoughts to jumpstart the writing process.* New York: Scholastic.

Rog, L.J. (1996). *Love of writing handbook.* Regina, SK, Canada: Regina Public Schools.

Rog, L.J. (2001). *Early literacy instruction in kindergarten.* Newark, DE: International Reading Association.

Rog, L.J. (2003). *Guided reading basics.* Markham, ON: Pembroke.

Rog, L.J., & Kropp, P. (2004). *The write genre.* Markham, ON, Canada: Pembroke.

Roser, N.L., & Bomer, K. (2005). Writing in primary classrooms: A teacher's story. In R. Indrisano & J.R. Paratore (Eds.), *Learning to write, writing to learn: Theory and research in practice* (pp. 26–39). Newark, DE: International Reading Association.

Routman, R. (1994). *Invitations: Changing as teachers and learners, K–12.* Portsmouth, NH: Heinemann.

Routman, R. (2005). *Writing essentials: Raising expectations and results while simplifying teaching.* Portsmouth, NH: Heinemann.

Schickedanz, J.A. (1998). What is developmentally appropriate practice in early literacy? Considering the alphabet. In S.B. Neuman & K.A. Roskos (Eds.), *Children achieving: Best practices in early literacy* (pp. 20–37). Newark, DE: International Reading Association.

Spandel, V. (1997). *Seeing with new eyes: A guidebook on teaching & assessing beginning writers.* Portland, OR: Northwest Regional Educational Laboratory.

Spandel, V. (2001). *Creating writers through 6-Trait writing assessment and instruction* (3rd ed.). New York: Longman.

Spandel, V. (2003). *Creating young writers: Using the six traits to enrich writing process in primary classrooms.* Upper Saddle River, NJ: Pearson Education.

Sulzby, E., Barnhart, J., & Hieshima, J. (1989). *Forms of writing and rereading from writing: A preliminary report* (Technical Report No. 20). Berkeley, CA: University of California, Center for the Study of Writing.

Tate, M. (2003). *Worksheets don't grow dendrites: 20 instructional strategies that engage the brain.* Thousand Oaks, CA: Corwin Press.

Teale, W.H., & Yokota, J. (2000). Foundations on the early literacy curriculum. In D.S. Strickland & L.M. Morrow (Eds.), *Beginning reading and writing* (pp. 3–22). Newark, DE: International Reading Association.

Vygotsky, L.S. (1978). *Mind in society: The development of higher psychological processes* (M. Cole, V. John-Steiner, S. Scribner, & E. Souberman, Eds. & Trans.). Cambridge, MA: Harvard University Press. (Original work published 1934)

Wilde, S. (1997). *What's a schwa sound anyway? A holistic guide to phonetics, phonics, and spelling.* Portsmouth, NH: Heinemann.

Children's Literature Cited

Barrett, J. (2001). *Things that are most in the world.* New York: Simon & Schuster.

Baylor, B. (1994). *The table where rich people sit.* New York: Athenuem.

Bunting, E. (1991). *Night tree.* San Diego, CA: Harcourt Brace.

Burleigh, R. (1997). *Hoops!* Ill. S.T. Johnson. San Diego, CA: Silver Whistle.

Cronin, D. (2000). *Click, clack, moo: Cows that type.* New York: Simon & Schuster.

Fletcher, R. (1997). *Twilight comes twice.* Ill. K. Kiesler. New York: Clarion Books.

Fox, M. (1996). *Feathers and fools.* Ill. N. Wilton. San Diego, CA: Harcourt Brace.

Gantos, J. (1980). *Rotten Ralph.* Boston: Houghton Mifflin.

Henkes, K. (1993). *Owen.* New York: Greenwillow.

Henkes, K. (1996). *Chrysanthemum.* New York: HarperTrophy.

King-Smith, D. (2001). *I love guinea pigs.* Ill. A. Jeram. Cambridge, MA: Candlewick.

Lester, H. (2002). *Hooway for Wodney Wat.* Boston: Houghton Mifflin.

MacDonald, R. (2003). *Achoo! Bang! Crash! A noisy alphabet*. Brookfield, CT: Roaring Book Press.

McCracken, R., & McCracken, M. (1988). *Halloween*. Winnipeg, MB, Canada: Peguis.

Munsch, R. (1982). *Murmel, Murmel, Murmel*. Toronto, ON: Annick Press.

Noble, T. (1992). *Meanwhile, back at the ranch*. New York: Puffin.

Numeroff, L.J. (1998). *If you give a pig a pancake*. New York: Scholastic.

Orav, E.R. (2001). *Sun fun*. Ill. L. Quach. Toronto, ON: Curriculum Plus.

Paulsen, G. (1993). *Dogteam*. Ill. R.W. Paulsen. New York: Delacorte.

Scieszka, J. (2001). *Baloney, Henry P.* Ill. L. Smith. New York: Viking.

Shannon, D. (1995). *The amazing Christmas extravaganza*. New York: Blue Sky Press.

Stanley, D. (1996). *Saving sweetness*. New York: Putnam.

Swanson, S.M. (2002). *The first thing my mama told me*. San Diego, CA: Harcourt.

Wood, A. (1990). *Quiet as a cricket*. Ill. D. Wood. Bridgemead, Swindon, England: Child's Play International.

Note. Page numbers followed by *f* or *t* indicate figures or tables, respectively.